THE CHRONICLE OF WORLD HISTORY

Charting the course of human history
from the earliest times to the present day

Original wallchart (1890) drawn by
Professor Edward Hull, MA, LLD, FRS

Additional text by
Gill Davies

STUDIO EDITIONS
LONDON

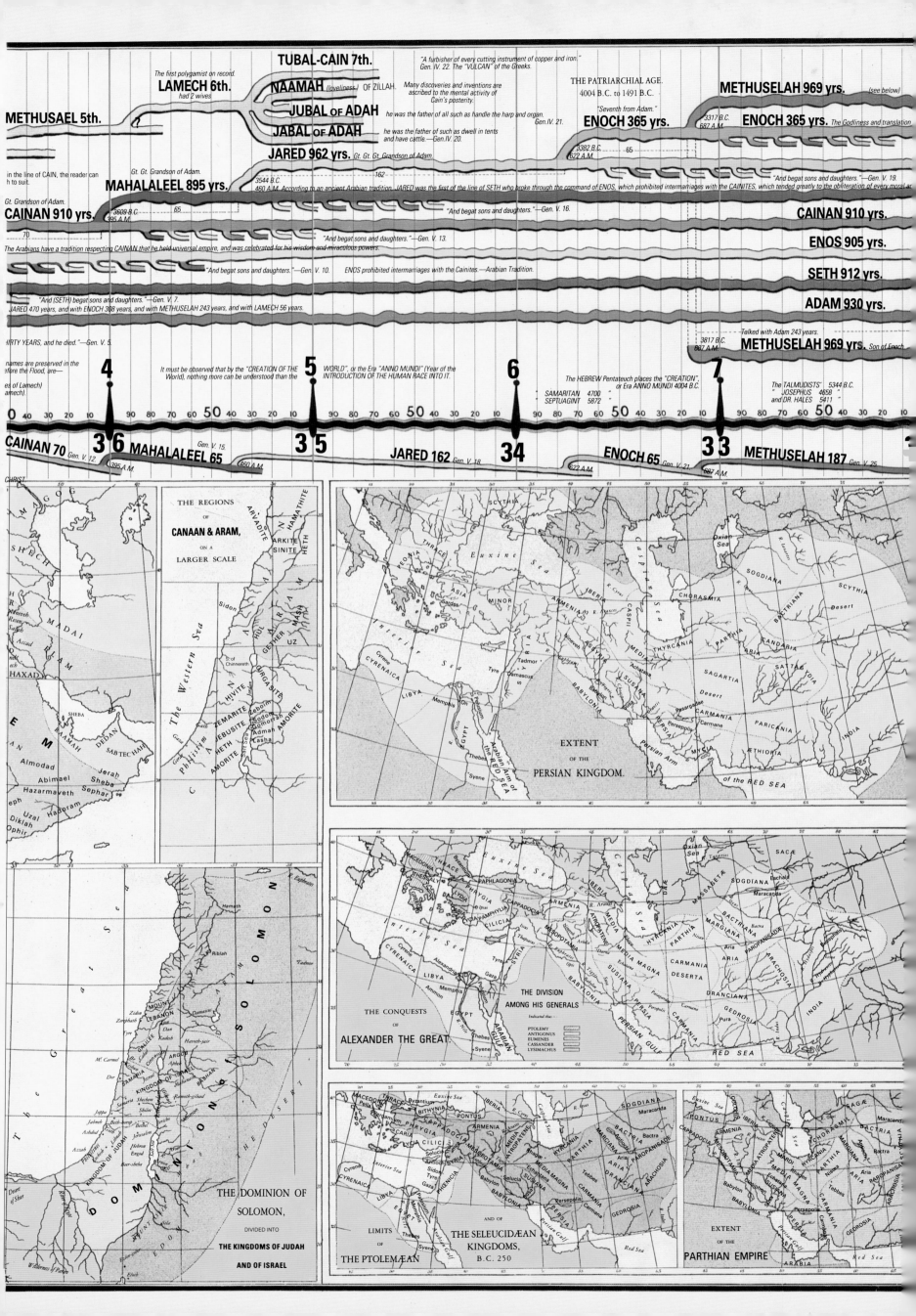

TUBAL-CAIN 7th.

"A furbisher of every cutting instrument of copper and iron."
Gen. IV. 22. The "VULCAN" of the Greeks.

The first polygamist on record.

NAAMAH (loveliness) OF ZILLAH.

THE PATRIARCHIAL AGE.
4004 B.C. to 1491 B.C.

METHUSELAH 969 yrs. (see below)

LAMECH 6th.
had 2 wives

Many discoveries and inventions are
ascribed to the mental activity of
Cain's posterity.

"Seventh from Adam."

JUBAL OF ADAH

METHUSAEL 5th.

he was the father of all such as handle the harp and organ.
Gen. IV. 21.

ENOCH 365 yrs.

3317 B.C.
687 A.M.

ENOCH 365 yrs. The Godliness and translation

JABAL OF ADAH

he was the father of such as dwell in tents
and have cattle.—Gen. IV. 20.

JARED 962 yrs. Gt. Gt. Gt. Grandson of Adam.

3382 B.C.
622 A.M.
65

in the line of CAIN, the reader can
h to suit.

Gt. Gt. Grandson of Adam.

MAHALALEEL 895 yrs.

3544 B.C.
460 A.M. According to an ancient Arabian tradition, JARED was the first of the line of SETH who broke through the command of ENOS, which prohibited intermarriages with the CAINITES, which tended greatly to the obliteration of every moral and

"And begat sons and daughters."—Gen. V. 19.

162

Gt. Grandson of Adam.

CAINAN 910 yrs.

3609 B.C.
395 A.M.
65

"And begat sons and daughters."—Gen. V. 16.

CAINAN 910 yrs.

70

The Arabians have a tradition respecting CAINAN that he held universal empire, and was celebrated for his wisdom and miraculous powers.

"And begat sons and daughters."—Gen. V. 13.

ENOS 905 yrs.

"And begat sons and daughters."—Gen. V. 10. ENOS prohibited intermarriages with the Cainites.—Arabian Tradition.

SETH 912 yrs.

"And (SETH) begat sons and daughters."—Gen. V. 7.

ADAM 930 yrs.

JARED 470 years, and with ENOCH 308 years, and with METHUSELAH 243 years, and with LAMECH 56 years.

Talked with Adam 243 years.

3817 B.C.
687 A.M.

HIRTY YEARS, and he died."—Gen. V. 5.

METHUSELAH 969 yrs. Son of Enoch.

names are preserved in the
before the Flood, are—

4

It must be observed that by the "CREATION OF THE
World), nothing more be understood than the

5

WORLD", or the Era "ANNO MUNDI" (Year of the
INTRODUCTION OF THE HUMAN RACE INTO IT.

6

The HEBREW Pentateuch places the "CREATION",
or Era ANNO MUNDI 4004 B.C.

7

es of Lamech)
amech.]

SAMARITAN 4700
SEPTUAGINT 5872

The TALMUDISTS' 5344 B.C.
JOSEPHUS 4658
and DR. HALES 5411 "

0 40 30 20 10 90 80 70 60 50 40 30 20 10 90 80 70 60 50 40 30 20 10 90 80 70 60 50 40 30 20 10 90 80 70 60 50 40 30 20 10

3 6
3 5
3 4
3 3

CAINAN 70 Gen. V. 12.

MAHALALEEL 65 Gen. V. 15.
395 A.M.

460 A.M.

JARED 162 Gen. V. 18.
622 A.M.

ENOCH 65 Gen. V. 21.
687 A.M.

METHUSELAH 187 Gen. V. 25.

THE REGIONS
OF
CANAAN & ARAM,
ON A
LARGER SCALE

EXTENT
OF THE
PERSIAN KINGDOM.

THE DOMINION
OF
SOLOMON,
DIVIDED INTO
THE KINGDOMS OF JUDAH
AND OF ISRAEL

THE CONQUESTS
OF
ALEXANDER THE GREAT

THE DIVISION
AMONG HIS GENERALS

Indicated thus—
PTOLEMY
ANTIGONUS
EUMENES
CASSANDER
LYSIMACHUS

LIMITS
OF
THE PTOLEMÆAN

AND OF
**THE SELEUCIDÆAN
KINGDOMS,**
B.C. 250

EXTENT
OF THE
PARTHIAN EMPIRE

Contents

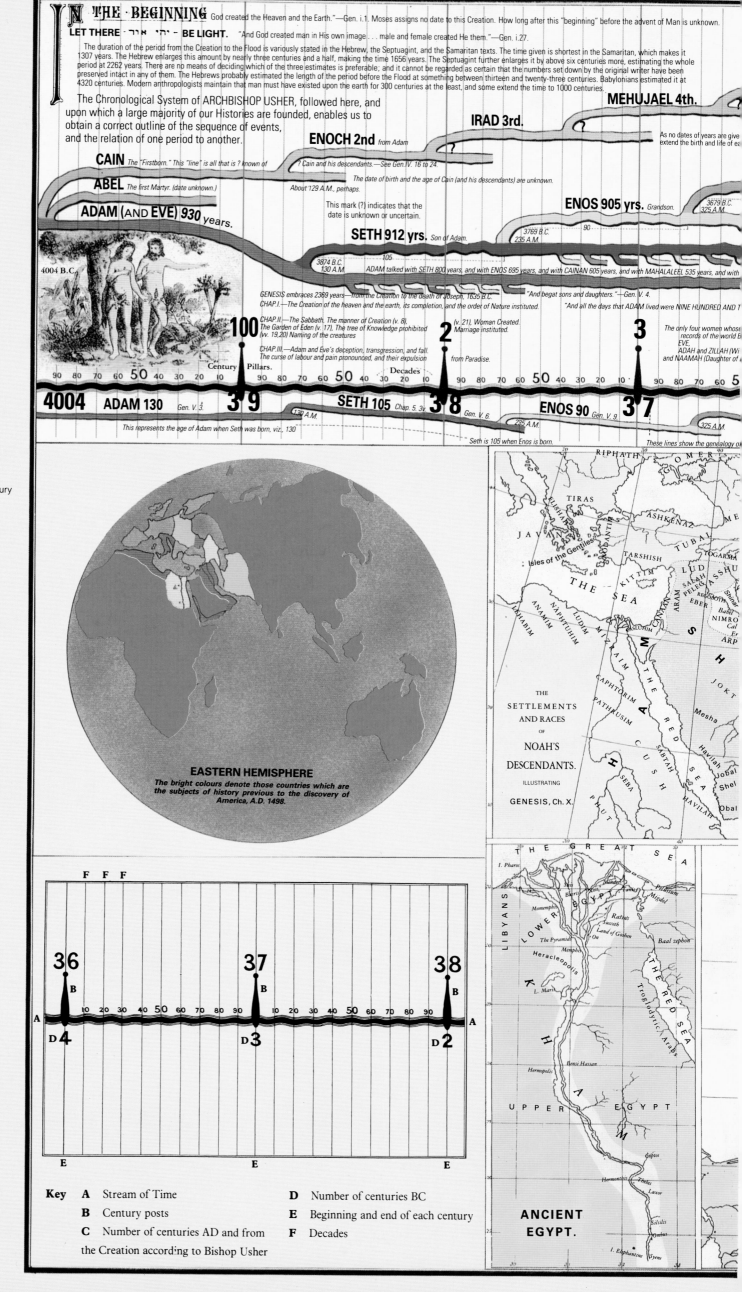

How to use this book

The Chronicle of World History is a book that follows the history of mankind through the course of time, showing what was happening concurrently in different places around the world. Drawn from an illustrated wallchart originally published in 1890, the information has been updated and extended to include the twentieth century and is illustrated with many pictures and informative charts to highlight important events and people.

The book can be used in three different ways:

You can simply turn over the pages of the time flow chart to look at two pages of history at a time.

Alternatively, as you go along you can pull open the left-hand pages, so that you can follow the stream of time across three pages at once.

More information Meanwhile, if you open up the right-hand pages, as indicated by the arrows in the margins, you will find a store of extra information, facts and figures about what was happening in the world at that time.

Follow the 'Stream of Time'

The black wavy line that runs runs continuously through the pull-out sections represents the **Stream of Time** and is marked with upright black pillars; these are **century posts,** dividing the Stream into 100-year sections. Large black figures *above* these posts denote the centuries from the Creation (according to Archbishop Usher in 1650) until the Birth of Christ and, thereafter, the centuries AD. Large black figures *below* the century posts denote the centuries BC.

Keeping track of time

Thin black perpendicular lines pass through the century posts to intersect the coloured **nation streams**; these help you to keep track of the changes of century. Long thin red lines indicate the **decades** which are also numbered in black on the Stream of Time.

The key

On the first page of the time-flow chart you will find a key which shows how the Stream of Time works. If you keep this page opened out you will be able to continue to refer to the key as you move forward in time.

The different nations

Variously coloured streams, running parallel to the Stream of Time, show the different nations, the width being proportional to the importance of the nation at that time. The name of each nation is printed in large black letters above the appropriate coloured stream. New streams indicate new nations, ending, dividing or being absorbed into another stream, according to the vagaries of history — with conquering nation's streams sweeping across the chart and becoming stouter with expansion.

Reigns and dynasties

The colours of the nation streams alter with each new dynasty, period or reign so a change of colour indicates the accession of a king, queen or emperor. Exact dates of accession or change are printed in small black figures where the colours alter. The number of years of rule are shown in larger figures, usually below the ruler's name.

Other guidelines

Biblical genealogy Thin streams *above* the main Stream of Time at the beginning of the chart show the family tree from Adam to Moses. Thin irregular or broken streams, set *below* the main Stream of Time, represent the genealogy of Christ.

The Roman Empire Ten large red crosses denote the ten great persecutions of the Christians. Red flags mark important battles.

The Crusades AD 1096-1270 are denoted by smaller red crosses.

Ecumenical Councils of the Church are shown by red circles.

Eminent people Coloured scrolls and strips at the top of the chart highlight eminent persons in literature, science and art and relate to their life spans. Where appropriate, small figures at each end indicate dates of birth and death.

The twentieth century

The chart element has been brought fully up to date — so far as space will allow — with the events of the twentieth century; a number of smaller countries have, of necessity, been omitted — and presidents and prime ministers replace kings and queens as the heads of state in most nations. (In major nations, presidents appear in upper halves and prime ministers in lower halves of coloured streams.)

Decade lines have been replaced by lines five years apart.

More information: Facts, figures and highlights

In the right-hand opening-out pages, indicated by arrows in the margins, you will find more detailed accounts of some of the events of the past, supplemented by charts and many informative facts and figures.

Dates and accuracy

Often opinions are divided as to dates; a question mark after any date or statement indicates that there is some uncertainty over the accuracy of this. The earlier pull-out sections of this book have been reproduced in part from an eighteenth-century wall chart and are therefore only as accurate as prevailing knowledge and understanding at that time allowed. While all reasonable steps have been taken to ensure the accuracy of the work and to provide additional information in the light of today's knowledge and to the best of their knowledge and belief all the text therein is correct, Studio Editions can accept no responsibility for the accuracy of fact or interpretation.

Published by Studio Editions
50 Eastcastle Street
London W1N 7AP

Wallchart first published around 1890 as *Deacon's Synchronological Chart of Universal History* by CW Deacon & Co., London.
Drawn by
Edward Hull, MA, LLD, FRS

ISNB 1 85170 969 X

Printed and bound in Singapore

Genesis: facts and theories

In 1650 Bishop Usher calculated the age of the earth from the evidence of the Old Testament. He decided that it must have been created at exactly 9am on 26 October, 4004 BC.

Scientists today, using the evidence of uranium dating, believe that the earth is some 3½ to 5 billion years old.

Tradition generally attributed the writing of Genesis to Moses. In 1753 the French physician Jean Astruc claimed it was drawn from two sources, as there were two names used for God (Yahweh and Elohim) and because many of the stories have two slightly different versions. In fact, close analysis reveals three distinct styles of writing and vocabulary.

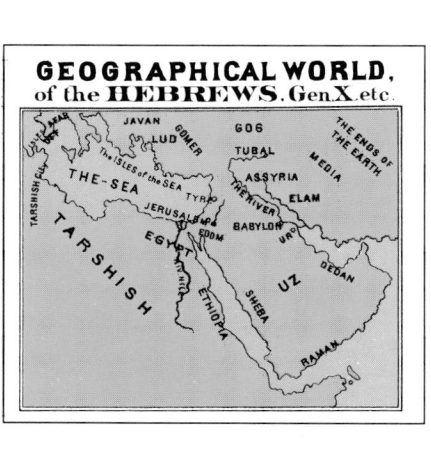

The name Genesis comes from the Greek word meaning generation, creation or birth. In the Hebrew Bible it is called 'Bereshith' meaning 'in the beginning'.

The Garden of Eden was set to the east of Palestine, at the source of the Tigris and the Euphrates.

The earliest human remains found in Palestine are of the hunter gatherers called the Natufian who lived there from 10,800 to 8500 BC.

We can relate the stories in Genesis to historic evidence from the Middle Bronze Age onwards (about 1750 BC).

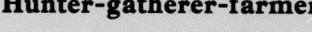

'Am I my brother's keeper?'

Abel, the shepherd, son of Adam, offered the first-born of his flock to the Lord God. Envious of his good standing on this account, his brother Cain, the tiller of soil, killed him in a jealous rage and became thus the first

Joseph

Scholars believe that the pharaoh in the story of Joseph was one of the Hyksos rulers. Evidently, the twenty shekels for which Joseph was sold was the average price for a slave in the 18th century BC.

Moreover, excavation has revealed that over half of the servants in one large Egyptian household at that time had Semitic names. This would seem to support the biblical account.

However, the revered status of the priest of On, whose daughter was given to Joseph in marriage, relates better to the time of Pharaoh Ikhnaton.

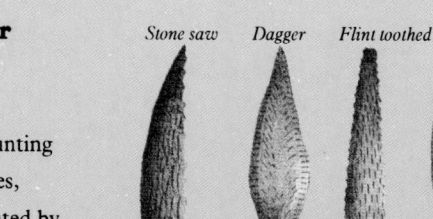

murderer in the Bible. God set a mark upon him and he was sent into exile to the land of Nod, east of Eden. Some theorists believe this story may refer to a vengeful nomadic tribe, possibly the Kenites, who sported a particular tattoo mark.

Human evolution: the fossil indications

Recent discoveries, particularly those in Africa, suggest that man has been in evidence for far longer than anthropologists earlier supposed. Moreover, since we now know that apes, in particular chimpanzees, do in fact create tools of a sort this is no longer a relevant distinction, and cranial capacity, skull shape and erect limbs are used for definition. Also, it appears that very primitive 'walking apes' in the early Pleistocene period virtually overlapped the existence of far more modern descendants. A good deal remains unknown and a true 'missing link' has yet to be found.

6 to 7 million years ago: Terrestrial ape-like mammals
4 to 5 million years ago: Bi-pedal hominids (Australopithecines) in East African Rift Valley and southern Africa
2.1 to 2.7 million years ago *Australopithecus africanus*
2 to 3 million years ago *Australopithecus aethiopicus* *Australopithecus balsei* *Australopithecus robustus* (The Australopithecines disappeared completely from the fossil record just over 1 million years ago)
2.5 million years ago *Homo habilis* in Africa Stone tools found in Ethiopia
1 to 2 million years ago (far earlier than previously believed) *Homo erectus* Man-made shelter in Olduvai Gorge, in Kenya, South Africa. Many stone tools used
850,000 BC European Paleolithic man
200,000 BC Middle Stone Age
120,000 BC Neanderthal man (cave dwellers) *Homo sapiens sapiens* in Africa and *Homo sapiens* in Asia
50,000 BC Human settlers arrive in Australia
30,000 BC Human settlement in the Americas

The Ice Age

There were, in fact, several ice ages but the one generally implied by this title is the Pleistocene ice age during which *homo sapiens* first appeared. It lasted about 2,000,000 years and ended (comparatively recently in geological time) some 10,000 years ago. Vast impenetrable ice sheets covered over 28 per cent of the land, including most of Europe, North America and Asia, and temperatures plummeted some 12°C (50°F). Woolly mammoth and reindeer grazed the sub-arctic vegetation but human beings were restricted to living in the equatorial regions until the glaciers gradually retreated.

Slowly the forests spread north, climatic conditions improved, land 'bridges' appeared which linked isolated islands into a single continental mainland, and the adaptable, inventive human race became more advanced and further widespread, creating better tools, hunting animals for meat and using fire to cook.

Hunter-gatherer-farmer

As the Paleolithic Age drew to a close, so agriculture began. Hunting continued, using axes, flint blades, spears and harpoons, supplemented by fishing and the gathering of plant, fruit and seed. But as human beings spread, large game became more scarce and in the new warmer climate, the domestication of animals and cultivation of cereals began.

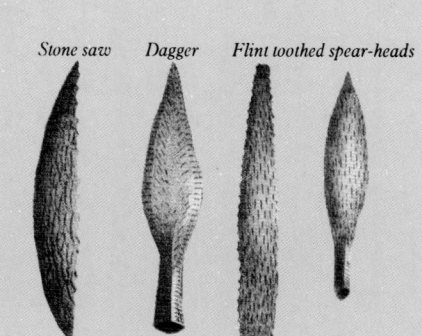

Stone saw *Dagger* *Flint toothed spear-heads*

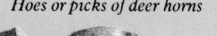

Hoes or picks of deer horns

Axe-hammer *Two-edged axe* *Hatchet-hammer*

Stone age family and implements

here is a Book extant called the "BOOK OF ENOCH", but generally
considered apocryphal.
Was perhaps written by some devout Christian of the first century."
—Ed. Robinson, D.D., Ed. Bi.Dic.

3130 B.C.
874 A.M.

From Adam to Moses there are only Five intervening links (with Kohath, Six). From "Creation" to Moses' death is 2553 years, so that through these Six intervening links the history of Man could have been brought down by "Tradition" from "Creation" to Moses' death, a period of 2553 years.

243   14

| ADAM, 687 yrs. to | | METHUSELAH, 628 y. to | | SHEM, 452 yrs. to | | ISAAC, 77 to | | LEVI, 70 y, to | | AMRAM, 61 to | MOSES |

ENOCH in Chap.V.24. JUDE (v.14) refers to Enoch as a prophet.

98   50   53   104 KOHATH. 42   58

3017 B.C.
987 A.M.

The Arabian name of ENOCH is EDRIS, and their traditions of him are
that he was an eminent astronomer, mathematician, and prophet of God.

"And Enoch walked with God 365 years, "and begat sons and daughters.—Gen. V. 22.
"And he was not, for God took him."—v.24.

JARED, 962 yrs.

MAHALALEEL, 895 yrs.

igious principle.

The marriage of brother and sister was common, until prohibited by the law of Moses in 1491 B.C.

CAINAN, 910 yrs.

B.C.
2769
1235
A.M.

"It is said of Seth and his posterity, that they were very good and virtuous, and very happy, without any considerable misfortunes for Seven generations."—Josephus.

2864 B.C.
1140 A.M.

"Seth and his posterity were the inventors of that peculiar sort of wisdom which is concerned with the heavenly bodies and their order."—Josephus.

2962 B.C.
1042 A.M.

NOAH, 950 yrs.   84 yrs.   talked with CAINAN 179 years, and with MAHALALEEL 234 years, and with JARED 366 yea

3474 B.C.
930 A.M.   Death of Adam. 126 yrs.

2948 B.C.
1056 A.M.   Lamech is the first man on record who died a natural death before his father (five years before).

LAMECH, 777 yrs.

And begat sons and daughters."—Gen. V. 30.

3130 B.C.
874 A.M.

METHUSELAH talks with SETH 355 years, and with ENOS 453 years, and with CAINAN 548 years, and with MAHALALEEL 603 years, and with JARED 735 years, and with ENOCH 300 years.

9   **10**   **11**   **12**

An old tradition says that Adam had 33 sons and
23 daughters.

A "Talent" was about 125 pounds Troy.
A "Talent" of Silver was worth about £353 11s. 10d.
A "Talent" of Gold was worth about £5075 15s. 7d.

"And begat sons and daughters."—Gen. V. 26.

This mark (?) indicates that the date
is unknown or uncertain.

"And all the days of

METHUSELAH were Nine
and nine years, and he die

LAMECH could talk with ADAM 56 years, and learn the story   of the Garden of Eden, etc. etc., an

90 80 70 50 40 30 20 10   90 80 70 50 40 30 20 10   90 80 70 50 40 30 20 10   90 80 70 50 40 30 20 10   90 80 70 50

31   **30**   **2 9**   **2 8**

LAMECH, 182   NOAH,

1056 A.M.

THE ROMAN EMPIRE

EUROPE, ETC.
IN THE NINTH CENTURY.

THE ROMAN EMPIRE
DIVIDED.

EUROPE
IN THE SIXTEENTH CENTURY.

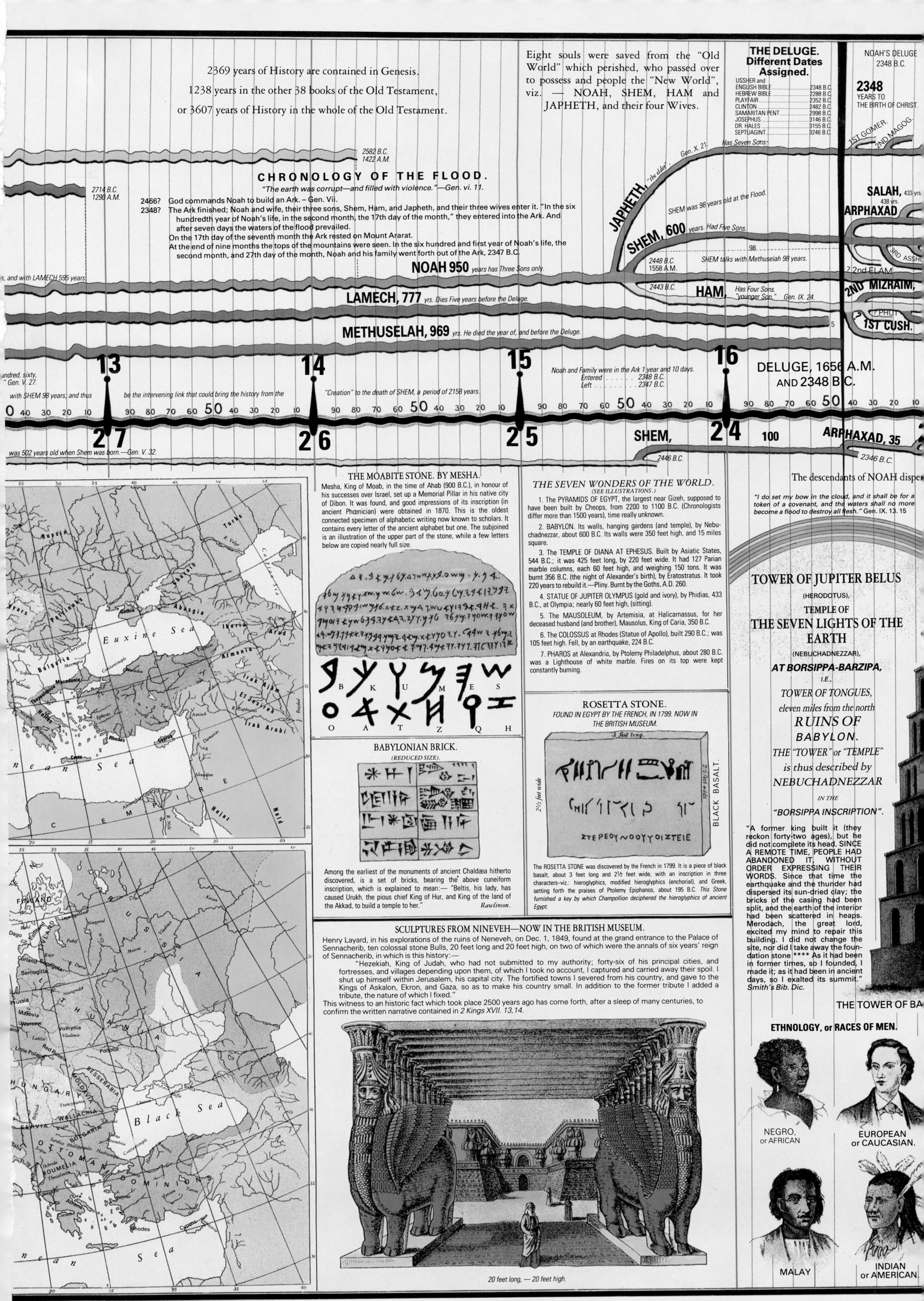

2369 years of History are contained in Genesis.

1238 years in the other 38 books of the Old Testament,

or 3607 years of History in the whole of the Old Testament.

Eight souls were saved from the "Old World" which perished, who passed over to possess and people the "New World", viz. — NOAH, SHEM, HAM and JAPHETH, and their four Wives.

THE DELUGE. Different Dates Assigned.

USSHER and ENGLISH BIBLE	2348 B.C.
HEBREW BIBLE	2288 B.C.
PLAYFAIR	2352 B.C.
CLINTON	2482 B.C.
SAMARITAN PENT	2998 B.C.
JOSEPHUS	3146 B.C.
DR. HALES	3155 B.C.
SEPTUAGINT	3246 B.C.

NOAH'S DELUGE 2348 B.C.

2348 YEARS TO THE BIRTH OF CHRIST.

1ST GOMER. 2ND MAGOG.

CHRONOLOGY OF THE FLOOD.

"The earth was corrupt—and filled with violence."—Gen. vi. 11.

2582 B.C. 1422 A.M.

2714 B.C. 1290 A.M.

2466? God commands Noah to build an Ark. – Gen. Vii.

2348? The Ark finished; Noah and wife, their three sons, Shem, Ham, and Japheth, and their three wives enter it. "In the six hundredth year of Noah's life, in the second month, the 17th day of the month," they entered into the Ark. And after seven days the waters of the flood prevailed.

On the 17th day of the seventh month the Ark rested on Mount Ararat.

At the end of nine months the tops of the mountains were seen. In the six hundred and first year of Noah's life, the second month, and 27th day of the month, Noah and his family went forth out of the Ark, 2347 B.C.

JAPHETH "the Elder". Has Seven Sons: Gen. X. 21.

SHEM was 98 years old at the Flood.

SHEM, 600 years. Had Five Sons.

NOAH 950 years has Three Sons only.

98.

2448 B.C. 1558 A.M. SHEM talks with Methuselah 98 years.

SALAH, 433 yrs. 438 yrs. ARPHAXAD

3RD ASSHUR

LAMECH, 777 yrs. Dies Five years before the Deluge.

2443 B.C. HAM Has Four Sons. "younger Son." Gen. IX. 24.

2 2nd ELAM

2ND MIZRAIM,

2 PHUT

METHUSELAH, 969 yrs. He died the year of, and before the Deluge.

1ST CUSH.

s, and with LAMECH 595 years.

13

14

15

Noah and Family were in the Ark 1 year and 10 days.
Entered . . . . 2348 B.C.
Left . . . . 2347 B.C.

16

DELUGE, 1656 A.M. AND 2348 B.C.

"Gen. V. 27.

with SHEM 98 years, and thus

be the intervening link that could bring the history from the

"Creation" to the death of SHEM, a period of 2158 years.

90 80 70 60 50 40 30 20 10

0 40 30 20 10 90 80 70 60 50 40 30 20 10 90 80 70 60 50 40 30 20 10 90 80 70 60 50

27 **26** **25** **24** 100 ARPHAXAD, 35

was 502 years old when Shem was born.—Gen. V. 32.

SHEM,

2446 B.C.

2346 B.C.

The descendants of NOAH disper[sed]

"I do set my bow in the cloud, and it shall be for a token of a covenant, and the waters shall no more become a flood to destroy all flesh." Gen. IX. 13. 15

THE MOABITE STONE. BY MESHA.

Mesha, King of Moab, in the time of Ahab (900 B.C.), in honour of his successes over Israel, set up a Memorial Pillar in his native city of Dibon. It was found, and good impressions of its inscription (in ancient Phœnician) were obtained in 1870. This is the oldest connected specimen of alphabetic writing now known to scholars. It contains every letter of the ancient alphabet but one. The subjoined is an illustration of the upper part of the stone, while a few letters below are copied nearly full size.

B K U M E S
O A T Z Q H

BABYLONIAN BRICK.

(REDUCED SIZE.)

Among the earliest of the monuments of ancient Chaldæa hitherto discovered, is a set of bricks, bearing the above cuneiform inscription, which is explained to mean:— "Beltis, his lady, has caused Urukh, the pious chief King of Hur, and King of the land of the Akkad, to build a temple to her." *Rawlinson.*

THE SEVEN WONDERS OF THE WORLD.

(SEE ILLUSTRATIONS.)

1. THE PYRAMIDS OF EGYPT, the largest near Gizeh, supposed to have been built by Cheops, from 2200 to 1100 B.C. (Chronologists differ more than 1500 years); time really unknown.

2. BABYLON. Its walls, hanging gardens (and temple), by Nebuchadnezzar, about 600 B.C. Its walls were 350 feet high, and 15 miles square.

3. The TEMPLE OF DIANA AT EPHESUS. Built by Asiatic States, 544 B.C.; it was 425 feet long, by 220 feet wide. It had 127 Parian marble columns, each 60 feet high, and weighing 150 tons. It was burnt 356 B.C. (the night of Alexander's birth), by Eratostratus. It took 220 years to rebuild it.—Pliny. Burnt by the Goths, A.D. 260.

4. STATUE OF JUPITER OLYMPUS (gold and ivory), by Phidias, 433 B.C., at Olympia; nearly 60 feet high, (sitting).

5. The MAUSOLEUM, by Artemisia, at Halicarnassus, for her deceased husband (and brother), Mausolus, King of Caria, 350 B.C.

6. The COLOSSUS at Rhodes (Statue of Apollo), built 290 B.C.; was 105 feet high. Fell, by an earthquake, 224 B.C.

7. PHAROS at Alexandria, by Ptolemy Philadelphus, about 280 B.C. was a Lighthouse of white marble. Fires on its top were kept constantly burning.

ROSETTA STONE.

FOUND IN EGYPT BY THE FRENCH, IN 1799. NOW IN THE BRITISH MUSEUM.

3 feet long.

2½ feet wide

BLACK BASALT.

The ROSETTA STONE was discovered by the French in 1799. It is a piece of black basalt, about 3 feet long and 2½ feet wide, with an inscription in three characters–viz.: hieroglyphics, modified hieroglyphics (enchorial), and Greek, setting forth the praises of Ptolemy Epiphanos, about 195 B.C. *This Stone furnished a key by which Champollion deciphered the hieroglyphics of ancient Egypt.*

TOWER OF JUPITER BELUS

(HERODOTUS),

TEMPLE OF THE SEVEN LIGHTS OF THE EARTH

(NEBUCHADNEZZAR),

AT BORSIPPA-BARZIPA,

I.E.

TOWER OF TONGUES,

eleven miles from the north

RUINS OF BABYLON.

THE "TOWER" or "TEMPLE"

is thus described by

NEBUCHADNEZZAR

IN THE

"BORSIPPA INSCRIPTION".

"A former king built it (they reckon forty-two ages), but he did not complete its head. SINCE A REMOTE TIME, PEOPLE HAD ABANDONED IT, WITHOUT ORDER EXPRESSING THEIR WORDS. Since that time the earthquake and the thunder had dispersed its sun-dried clay; the bricks of the casing had been split, and the earth of the interior had been scattered in heaps. Merodach, the great lord, excited my mind to repair this building. I did not change the site, nor did I take away the foundation stone **** As it had been in former times, so I founded, I made it; as it had been in ancient days, so I exalted its summit." *Smith's Bib. Dic.*

THE TOWER OF BA[BEL]

SCULPTURES FROM NINEVEH—NOW IN THE BRITISH MUSEUM.

Henry Layard, in his explorations of the ruins of Neneveh, on Dec. 1, 1849, found at the grand entrance to the Palace of Sennacherib, ten colossal stone Bulls, 20 feet long and 20 feet high, on two of which were the annals of six years' reign of Sennacherib, in which is this history:—

"Hezekiah, King of Judah, who had not submitted to my authority; forty-six of his principal cities, and fortresses, and villages depending upon them, of which I took no account, I captured and carried away their spoil. I shut up himself within Jerusalem, his capital city. The fortified towns I severed from his country, and gave to the Kings of Askalon, Ekron, and Gaza, so as to make his country small. In addition to the former tribute I added a tribute, the nature of which I fixed."

This witness to an historic fact which took place 2500 years ago has come forth, after a sleep of many centuries, to confirm the written narrative contained in *2 Kings XVII. 13,14.*

20 feet long, — 20 feet high.

ETHNOLOGY, or RACES OF MEN.

NEGRO, or AFRICAN.

EUROPEAN or CAUCASIAN.

MALAY

INDIAN or AMERICAN.

The Creation Story: according to Genesis

In the beginning …
'God created the heaven and the earth.
And the earth was without form, and
void; and darkness was upon the face
of the deep. And the spirit of God
moved across the face of the waters.'

The first day
The division of light from darkness:
The creation of Day and Night.

The second day
The creation of the firmament:
The division of the waters which were
under the firmament from the waters
which were *above* the firmament.
God called the firmament Heaven.

The third day
The gathering of the waters to create
the dry land. God called the waters the
Seas and the dry land Earth. God made
grass, flower, fruit tree and seed.

The fourth day
The creation of lights in the firmament
—the sun, the moon and the stars: for
division of night from day, for signs, for
seasons, and for days and years.

The fifth day
God made whales and every moving
creature in the waters and winged fowl
to fly above the earth in the firmament.

The sixth day
God made the beasts of the earth, and
cattle, and every thing that creepeth
upon the earth. God made man in His
own image, to have dominion over the
fish of the sea and the fowl of the air,
and over the cattle and all the earth,
and over every creeping thing upon the
earth. God saw everything he had
made, and, behold, it was very good.

The seventh day
God ended his work and rested.
God blessed the seventh day and made
it holy.

Dinosaur remains
It was 1822 when Mary Anne Mantell discovered the first fossils to be recognized
as dinosaur remains — by her husband, Dr Gideon Mantell, a pioneering geologist
and paleontologist. Because the teeth resembled those of an iguana lizard the
dinosaur was named iguanadon. The discovery aroused a good deal of interest and
excitement and many other geologists set out to uncover further fossilized remains.

The periods described cover many millions of years with vast changes over the whole globe and this chart can give only a very brief impression of the most significant factors.

		Development of early life	Conditions on Earth	Flora and fauna
Cryptozoic	**TIME OF SECRET OR HIDDEN LIFE**	**Pre-Cambrian** — Primitive life-forms appear: simple marine life, soft-bodied animals and microscopic plants; algae and fungi	**4,550,000,000 years ago** — Semi-molten surface of the earth slowly forms into a crust. Atmosphere, seas and continental land masses form.	
Palaeozoic	**TIME OF EARLY OR ANCIENT LIFE**	**Cambrian** — Primitive arthropods, molluscs, worms and sponges; trilobites dominate	**570,000,000 years ago** — Large continents and shallow seas which gradually advance over much of the land, leaving clusters of islands.	
		Ordovician — Marine invertebrates: coral, starfish, clams. The first primitive fish; floating forms and graptolites	**500,000,000 years ago** — Many changes in distribution and height of both land and sea. Troughs and mountains form. Volcanic activity	
		Silurian — Plant life emerges on land	**440,000,000 years ago** — Widespread volcanic activity and mountain building. Deserts, landlocked seas and salt deposits formed; warm shallow seas and coral reefs.	
		Devonian — Abundant fish; freshwater fish and first primitive amphibians (lungfish) and sharks appear. Scale trees, tree ferns and horsetails on land. Trilobites and graptolites decline	**395,000,000 years ago** — Coral reefs; red sand and mud deposits. Convulsive mountain building alters continents; warping of earth's crust and changing seaways. Warm temperatures and arid deserts	
		Carboniferous — Lush forests and giant insects on land. Amphibians lay eggs on land.	**345,000,000 years ago** — River deltas build; tropical seas become swamp and forest (coal deposits). High mountain chains form; vast deserts in northern globe. Two main continents. Areas near to South Pole under repeated glaciation.	
		Permian — Land and freshwater reptiles — herbivorous and carnivorous; many more vertebrates; modern insects develop; first mammal-like reptiles. Coal forest plants decline; primitive conifers replace them	**280,000,000 years ago** — Violent volcanic activity; very warm; many deserts; earth's surface dries out. Extreme climatic contrasts: coral reefs fringe deserts; vast inland salt lakes; glaciers in the south. Land masses split and move to present positions.	
Mesozoic	**TIME OF MIDDLE LIFE**	**Triassic** — Large marine, two-footed and winged reptiles; ammonites; first dinosaurs	**225,000,000 years ago** — Continents become stable; seas flood into parts of Eurasia and North America. Desert conditions continue; wet and dry seasons alternate.	
		Jurassic — Dinosaurs dominate; large reptiles; primitive birds with teeth and small mammals appear	**195,000,000 years ago** — More uniform climate and no glaciation, even at the poles. Less physical disturbance in Europe but much in North America.	
		Cretaceous — Dinosaurs continue to evolve in many forms, some to a gigantic size, but then disappear. Many more mammals (placental and marsupial). Snakes, beaked birds, modern trees and flora develop	**136,000,000 years ago** — Mild climates everywhere. Vast expansion of seas and mountain building (the Andes and the Rockies) and submarine volcanic activity. Chalk deposits. Temperatures gradually cool	
Caenozoic	**TIME OF RECENT LIFE**	**Tertiary** — Mammals dominate the earth and bony fish the sea; large running and browsing mammals. Rise of flowering plants. Development of man-like apes	**65,000,000 years ago** — Violent volcanic activity. The Alps, Pyrenees, and Carpathians rise. Seas retreat. Continental uplift creates drier climates; forests mutate into prairies	
		Quarternary — Many mammals flourish but then become extinct, including mammoths, woolly rhinoceros and sabre-toothed tigers. Grazing mammals; whales and apes. Early man appears	**1,500,000 years ago** — Climatic fluctuation, with attendant changes in sea levels. Much colder: Continental ice sheets up to 10,000 feet (over 3,000 metres) thick across northern hemisphere; tundra and steppe conditions; deep lakes and deciduous forests	

Flora and fauna columns: Seaweed and invertebrates | Fish | Plants on land | Amphibians | Reptiles | Mammals | Birds | Man

Other flood legends

Assyria
According to the epic of Gilgamesh (7th century BC but probably repeating a much earlier original): Ut-Napishtim builds a vessel and rescues his family, craftsmen and 'the seed of all living creatures' from a flood which submerges the earth.

Sumerian version
King Ziusudra escapes in a giant ship — built on the instructions of one god who has taken pity on him — from a flood sent by the other gods.

Late Babylonian
Cronus commands Xisuthros to build a ship and to take family, friends and animals aboard to avoid an imminent flood. After the flood Xisuthros releases birds three times to see if the water has sunk but they do not return. So, with three others, he leaves the ship as a sacrifice — it eventually returns to Babylon.

Greece
Zeus decides to destroy humanity but King Deucalion and his wife Pyrrha escape in an ark which finally comes to rest on Mount Parnassus. Zeus is appeased and allows Deucalion to increase the human race. He throws stones over his shoulders which turn into men while those thrown by Pyrrha become women.

India
In 1500-1000 BC a great flood is mentioned in Vedic hymns. In 600 BC the story of Manu tells how he is advised by a fish of an imminent flood. Manu builds a ship which is pulled to safety by the fish. A sacrifice of butter and milk Manu makes on the mountain side creates a woman who becomes the mother of mankind.

China
To counteract the effects of a great deluge, Kun steals from heaven a mystical piece of earth from which plants grow. But it is his son the great Yü, the Tamer of the Flood, who succeeds in organising the water animals, especially dragons and tortoises, to drag their tails along particular routes and so create channels through which the water disperses — leaving the earth fertile and supportive of human kind.

Similar legends can be found in places as widely distributed as Australia, America, Rumania, Wales, Polynesia, Alaska and eastern Russia but are scarcely in evidence at all in Egypt or the rest of Africa.

The Great Pyramid at Gizeh

Completed in about 2500 BC, the Great Pyramid of Cheops was originally 147 metres (481 feet) high — higher than the spire of Salisbury Cathedral — when all the stones were still in place. It contains some 2½ million blocks of limestone, some of which weigh 15 tons each, and it probably took 4,000 builders and masons at least 20 to 30 years to build.

Its proportions and measurements are incredibly accurate; the sides are orientated to the four compass points to within one tenth of a degree. Just how it was constructed no-one really knows; nor do we know if it was actually intended to be a tomb for King Cheops.

Inside are many corridors and chambers, including what are now called the Queen's Chamber, the King's Chamber (which houses an empty and lidless red granite sarcophagus) and the Grand Gallery, over 8 metres (26 feet) high and 47 metres (153 feet) long.

The Seven Wonders of the World

The Pyramids of Egypt near Gizeh	built by Cheops	2500-1100 BC
Hanging Gardens & Temple of Babylon	built by Nebuchadnezzar	6000 BC
The Temple of Diana at Ephesus	built by Asiatic States	544 BC
Statue of Jupiter Olympus at Olympia	built by Phidias	433 BC
The Mausoleum at Halicarnassus	built by Artemisia	350 BC
The Colossus at Rhodes	builder unknown	290 BC
The Pharos lighthouse at Alexandria	built by Ptolemy Philadelphus	280 BC

Early cultures worldwide

Europe	The Americas	Asia and Oceania	Africa
3200 BC Megalithic standing stones Wheeled vehicles appear	**3200 BC** First cultivation of maize	**3250-3100 BC** First writing and pictograms used in Mesopotamia; cuneiform script used	**3400 BC** Walled towns in Egypt
…0 BC Products are made in metal Walled citadels in Mediterranean areas	**2800 BC** Farming communities near Amazon		**3100-3000 BC** Egyptian capital at Memphis First hieroglyphics used
	2600 BC Peruvian temple mounds	**3000-2700 BC** Stone tools used in Australia Ploughs, silk weaving, and bronze artefacts in China	
2900 BC Corded ware pottery made in north			**2700-2500 BC** Egyptian Old Kingdom Stepped pyramid built at Saqqara Great Pyramid built at Gizeh
2700-2200 BC 56 pits dug in circle at Stonehenge	**2500 BC** Improved maize cultivation; more permanent and larger villages Stone tools and loom weaving in South America. Irrigation methods develop and trade over vast distances	**2500 BC** Walled settlements and wheel thrown pottery in China Urban growth and first cotton cloth in Indus Valley City states and palaces in Mesopotamia and the Levant. Royal graves at Ur Domesticated animals in S.E. Asia 4-wheeled war wagons (Mesopotamia)	**2040 BC** Egyptian Middle Kingdom established
2500 BC Beaker folk in western Europe			The dessication of the Sahara concentrates agriculture and development in the Nile Valley and the savanna grasslands. Hunting and gathering continue south of the Equator, with low levels of population generally throughout Africa.
2300 BC European Bronze Age begins	**2300-2000 BC** Ceramics in Meso-America and Peru		
2000 BC Stone circles erected at Stonehenge	**2000 BC** Early Eskimos use flint and small stone tools	**2300 BC** First Old World Empire	

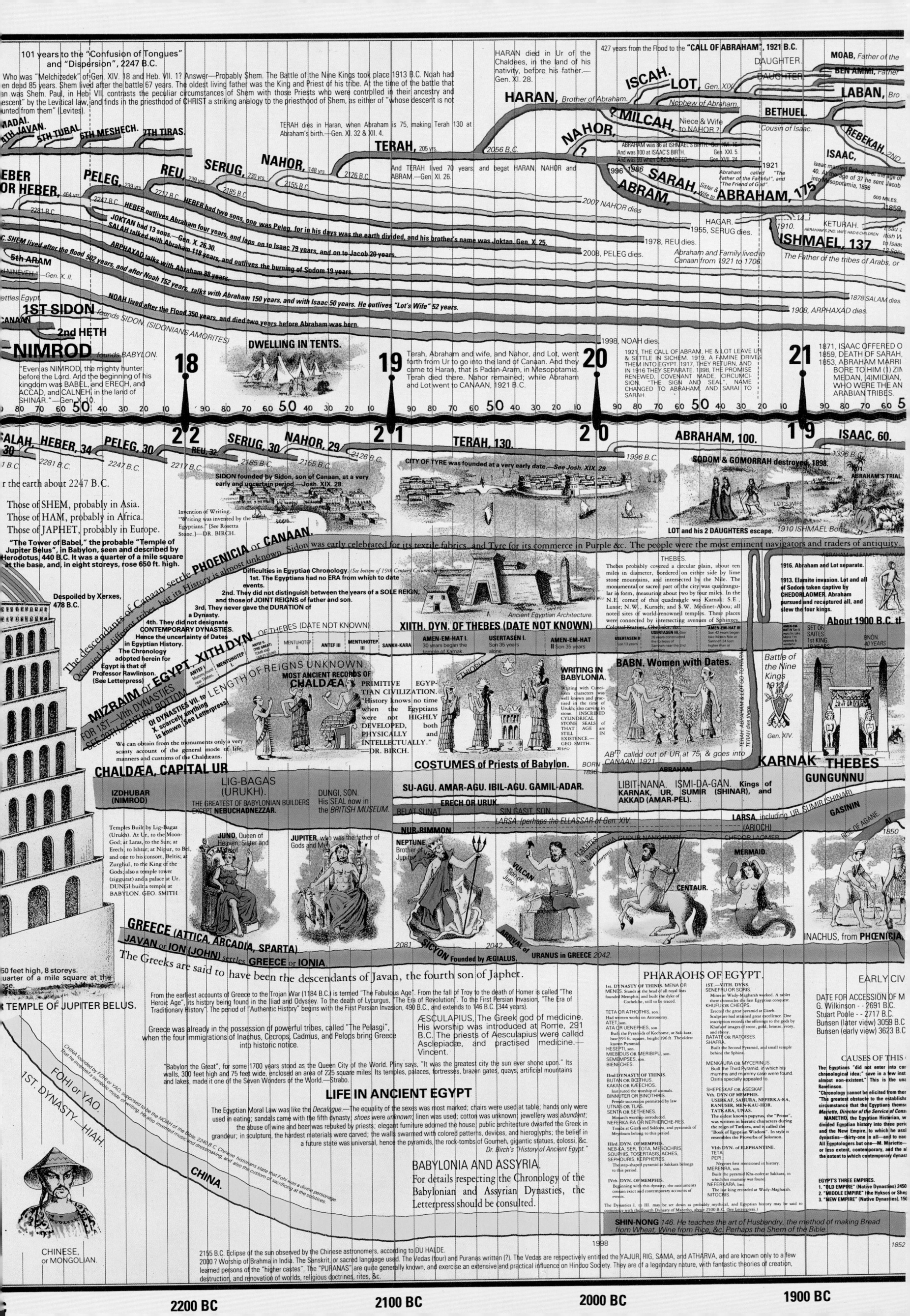

101 years to the "Confusion of Tongues" and "Dispersion", 2247 B.C.

Who was "Melchizedek" of Gen. XIV. 18 and Heb. VII. 1? Answer—Probably Shem. The Battle of the Nine Kings took place 1913 B.C. Noah had been dead 85 years. Shem lived after the battle 67 years. The oldest living father was Shem, and Priest of his tribe. At the time of the battle that an was Shem. Paul, in Heb. VII. contrasts the peculiar circumstances of Shem with those Priests who were controlled in their ancestry and escent" by the Levitical law, and finds in the priesthood of CHRIST a striking analogy to the priesthood of Shem, as either of "whose descent is not unted from them" (Levites).

HARAN died in Ur of the Chaldees, in the land of his nativity, before his father.—Gen. XI. 28.

427 years from the Flood to the "CALL OF ABRAHAM", 1921 B.C.

ISCAH. LOT, Gen. XIX. Nephew of Abraham.
DAUGHTER. MOAB, Father of the
DAUGHTER. BEN AMMII, Father
LABAN, Bro
HARAN, Brother of Abraham.
NAHOR.
MILCAH, Niece & Wife to NAHOR?
BETHUEL, Cousin of Isaac.
REBEKAH, 2ND

TERAH dies in Haran, when Abraham is 75, making Terah 130 at Abraham's birth.—Gen. XI. 32 & XII. 1.

MADAI.
4TH JAVAN. 5TH TUBAL. 6TH MESHECH. 7TH TIRAS.

TERAH, 205 yrs. 2056 B.C.

ABRAHAM was 86 at ISHMAEL'S BIRTH. Gen. XVI. 16. And was 100 at ISAAC'S BIRTH. Gen. XXI. 5. And was 99 when CIRCUMCISED.

And TERAH lived 70 years and begat HARAN, NAHOR and ABRAM.—Gen. XI. 26.

ISAAC, 2ND

Isaac married Rebekah at the age of 40. At the age of 37 he sent Jacob into Mesopotamia, 1896.

EBER OR HEBER.
PELEG, 239 yrs. 2217 B.C.
REU, 239 yrs. 2185 B.C.
SERUG, 230 yrs. 2155 B.C.
NAHOR, 148 yrs. 2126 B.C.
TERAH, 205 yrs.

ABRAM. SARAH, Sister & Wife to ABRAHAM, 175
Abraham called "The Father of the Faithful", and "The Friend of God".
996 1986 1921

HAGAR. KETURAH. 1910 2ND WIFE HAD CHILDREN
1955, SERUG dies.
ISHMAEL, 137
The Father of the tribes of Arabs, or

HEBER, 464 yrs. 2247 B.C. 2281 B.C.
HEBER outlives Abraham four years, and laps on to Isaac 79 years.
JOKTAN had 13 sons.—Gen. X. 26,30.
SALAH talked with Abraham 118 years.
ARPHAXAD talks with Abraham 88 years.

Abraham and Family lived in Canaan from 1921 to 1706

1978, REU dies.
2008, PELEG dies.
1878 SALAM dies
1908, ARPHAXAD dies

5th ARAM
SHEM lived after the flood 502 years, and after Noah 152 years, talks with Abraham 150 years, and with Isaac 50 years. He outlives "Lot's Wife" 52 years.

NOAH lived after the Flood 350 years, and died two years before Abraham was born.

1998, NOAH dies.

1ST SIDON founds SIDON (SIDONIANS AMORITES)

2nd HETH

NIMROD founds BABYLON.

18

19

20

21

DWELLING IN TENTS.

Terah, Abraham and wife, and Nahor, and Lot, went forth from Ur to go into the land of Canaan. And they came to Haran, that is Padan-Aram, in Mesopotamia. Terah died there. Nahor remained; while Abraham and Lot went to CANAAN, 1921 B.C.

1921, THE CALL OF ABRAM, HE & LOT LEAVE UR & SETTLE IN SICHEM. 1919. A FAMINE DRIVES THEM INTO EGYPT. 1917. THEY RETURN. AND IN 1916 THEY SEPARATE. 1898, THE PROMISE RENEWED. COVENANT MADE. CIRCUMCISION. "THE SIGN AND SEAL". NAME CHANGED TO ABRAHAM AND SARAI TO SARAH.

1871, ISAAC OFFERED O 1859, DEATH OF SARAH. 1853, ABRAHAM MARRI BORE TO HIM (1) ZIN MEDAN, (4)MIDIAN, WHO WERE THE ARABIAN TRIBES.

"Even as NIMROD, the mighty hunter before the Lord. And the beginning of his kingdom was BABEL, and ERECH, and ACCAD, and CALNEH in the land of SHINAR."—Gen. X.

50 10 20 30 40 30 20 10 **50** 40 30 20 70 80 90 60 **50** 40 30 20 10 90 80 70 60 **50** 40 30 20 10 90 80 70 60 **5**

SALAH, 30 HEBER, 34 PELEG, 30
22
REU, 32 SERUG, 30 NAHOR, 29
21
TERAH, 130.
20
ABRAHAM, 100.
19
ISAAC, 60.

2281 B.C. 2247 B.C. 2217 B.C. 2185 B.C. 2156 B.C. 2126 B.C. 1996 B.C. 1996 B.C.

r the earth about 2247 B.C.

Those of SHEM, probably in Asia.
Those of HAM, probably in Africa.
Those of JAPHET, probably in Europe.

"The Tower of Babel," the probable "Temple of Jupiter Bélus", in Babylon, seen and described by Herodotus, 440 B.C. It was a quarter of a mile square at the base, and, in eight storeys, rose 650 ft. high.

Despoiled by Xerxes, 478 B.C.

SIDON founded by Sidon, son of Canaan, at a very early and uncertain period.—Josh. XIX. 28.

Invention of Writing. "Writing was invented by the Egyptians." [See Rosetta Stone.]—DR. BIRCH.

CITY OF TYRE was founded at a very early date.—See Josh. XIX. 29.

1996 B.C.

SODOM & GOMORRAH destroyed, 1898. 1996 B.C.
LOT'S WIFE
LOT and his 2 DAUGHTERS escape. 1910 ISHMAEL Born

ABRAHAM'S TRIAL.

The descendants of Canaan settle PHOENICIA or CANAAN. Sidon was early celebrated for its textile fabrics, and Tyre for its commerce in Purple &c. The people were the most eminent navigators and traders of antiquity.

The descendants of Canaan occupied by different tribes, but its History is almost unknown

Difficulties in Egyptian Chronology. (See bottom of 19th Century Column.)
1st. The Egyptians had no ERA from which to date events.
2nd. They did not distinguish between the years of a SOLE REIGN, and those of JOINT REIGNS of father and son.
3rd. They never gave the DURATION of a Dynasty.
4th. They did not designate CONTEMPORARY DYNASTIES. Hence the uncertainty of Dates in Egyptian History. The Chronology adopted herein for Egypt is that of Professor Rawlinson. (See Letterpress)

THEBES.
Thebes probably covered a circular plain, about ten miles in diameter, bordered on either side by lime stone mountains, and intersected by the Nile. The monumental or sacred part of the city was quadrangular in form, measuring about two by four miles. In the N.E. corner of this quadrangle was Karnak; S.E., Luxor; N.W., Kurneh; and S.W. Medinet-Abou; all noted sites of world-renowned temples. These places were connected by intersecting avenues of Sphinxes, Colossal Statues, Obelisks, &c.

1916. Abraham and Lot separate.

1913. Elamite invasion. Lot and all of Sodom taken captive by CHEDORLAOMER. Abraham pursued and recaptured all, and slew the four kings.

About 1900 B.C. th

MIZRAIM or EGYPT XITH DYN OF THEBES (DATE NOT KNOWN)

XIITH. DYN. OF THEBES (DATE NOT KNOWN)

FOR 1ST—VIth DYNASTIES SEE 20TH CENTURY BOTTOM

OF DYNASTIES VII. X. scarcely anything is known. LENGTH OF REIGNS UNKNOWN. (See Letterpress)

We can obtain from the monuments only a very scanty account of the general mode of life, manners and customs of the Chaldæans.

ANTEF I MENTUHOTEP II ANTEF II ANTEF III MENTUHOTEP III SANKH-KARA

AMEN-EM-HAT I. 30 years began the temple of Karnak.
USERTASEN I. Son 35 years alone.
AMEN-EM-HAT II Son 35 years.
USERTASEN II Son 13 years
AMEN-EM-HAT III, Son 26 years distinguished at the fortress of Samhoud near the 2nd
USERTASEN III, Son reigned
Battle of the Nine Kings 1913
Gen. XIV.

MOST ANCIENT RECORDS OF CHALDÆA

PRIMITIVE EGYPTIAN CIVILIZATION. "History knows no time when the Egyptians were not HIGHLY DEVELOPED, both PHYSICALLY and INTELLECTUALLY." —DR. BIRCH.

WRITING IN BABYLONIA. Writing with Cuneiform characters was well known and practised in the time of Urukh; also carving in stone. INSCRIBED CYLINDRICAL STONE SEALS OF THAT AGE are STILL IN EXISTENCE.—GEO. SMITH.

BABN. Women with Dates.

KARNAK THEBES
GUNGUNNU

CHALDÆA, CAPITAL UR

LIG-BAGAS (URUKH).
IZDHUBAR (NIMROD)
THE GREATEST OF BABYLONIAN BUILDERS EXCEPT NEBUCHADNEZZAR.
DUNGI, SON. His SEAL now in BRITISH MUSEUM.
BELAT SUNAT

SU-AGU. AMAR-AGU. IBIL-AGU. GAMIL-ADAR.
ERECH OR URUK. SIN GASIT SON
NUR-RIMMON
LARSA (perhaps the ELLASSAR of Gen. XIV.

LIBIT-NANA. ISMI-DA-GAN. Kings of KARNAK, UR, SUMIR (SHINAR), and AKKAD (AMAR-PEL).

LARSA including UR, SUMIR (SHINAR) (ARIOCH)
GASININ
RISE OF AGANE

Temples Built by Lig-Bagas (Urukh). At Ur, to the Moon-God; at Laras, to the Sun; at Erech, to Ishtar; at Nipur, to Bel, and one to his consort, Beltis; at Zurghul, to the King of the Gods; also a temple tower (ziggurat) and a palace at Ur. DUNGI built a temple at BABYLON. GEO. SMITH

JUNO, Queen of Heaven, Sister and Wife of
JUPITER, who was the father of Gods and Men
NEPTUNE Brother of Jupiter
VULCAN Son of Juno
CENTAUR.
MERMAID.
CHEDOR-LAOMER

ELAMITES IN BABYLONIA. KUDUR-NANKHUNDI

GREECE (ATTICA, ARCADIA, SPARTA)
JAVAN or ION (JOHN) settles GREECE or IONIA
The Greeks are said to have been the descendants of Javan, the fourth son of Japhet.

SICYON Founded by ÆGIALUS
ARRIVAL of URANUS in GREECE 2042
INACHUS, from PHŒNICIA

50 feet high, 8 storeys. quarter of a mile square at the ase.

TEMPLE OF JUPITER BELUS.

From the earliest accounts of Greece to the Trojan War (1184 B.C.) is termed "The Fabulous Age". From the fall of Troy to the death of Homer is called "The Heroic Age", its history being found in the Iliad and Odyssey. To the death of Lycurgus, "The Era of Revolution". To the First Persian Invasion, "The Era of Traditionary History". The period of "Authentic History" begins with the First Persian Invasion, 490 B.C., and extends to 146 B.C. (344 years).

ÆSCULAPIUS, The Greek god of medicine. His worship was introduced at Rome, 291 B.C. The priests of Aesculapius were called Asclepiadæ, and practised medicine.—Vincent.

Greece was already in the possession of powerful tribes, called "The Pelasgi", when the four immigrations of Inachus, Cecrops, Cadmus, and Pelops bring Greece into historic notice.

"Babylon the Great", for some 1700 years stood as the Queen City of the World. Pliny says, "It was the greatest city the sun ever shone upon." Its walls, 300 feet high and 75 feet wide, enclosed an area of 225 square miles. Its temples, palaces, fortresses, brazen gates, quays, artificial mountains and lakes, made it one of the Seven Wonders of the World.—Strabo.

LIFE IN ANCIENT EGYPT

The Egyptian Moral Law was like the Decalogue.—The equality of the sexes was most marked; chairs were used at table; hands only were used in eating; sandals came with the fifth dynasty, shoes were unknown; linen was used; cotton was unknown; jewellery was abundant; the abuse of wine and beer was rebuked by priests; elegant furniture adorned the house; public architecture dwarfed the Greek in grandeur; in sculpture, the hardest materials were carved; the walls swarmed with colored patterns, devices, and hieroglyphs; the belief in a future state was universal, hence the pyramids, the rock-tombs of Gourneh, gigantic statues, colossi, &c. Dr. Birch's "History of Ancient Egypt."

BABYLONIA AND ASSYRIA.
For details respecting the Chronology of the Babylonian and Assyrian Dynasties, the Letterpress should be consulted.

CHINA founded by FOHI or YAO. "supposed to be the NOAH of the Bible."

FOHI or YAO.
1ST DYNASTY—HIAH.
CHINA.

CHINESE, or MONGOLIAN.

PHARAOHS OF EGYPT.

1st. DYNASTY OF THINIS. MENA OR MENES. Stands at the head of all royal lists founded Memphis, and built the dyke of Cochelche, will to be traced.
TETA OR ATHOTHIS, son. Had written works on Astronomy.
ATET, son.
ATA OR UENEPHES, son. Built the Pyramids of Kochome, at Sak-kara; base 394 ft. square, height 196 ft. The oldest known Pyramid.
HESEPTI, son.
MIEBIDUS OR MERIBIPU, son.
SEMEMPSES, son.
BIENECHES.

IInd DYNASTY OF THINIS.
BUTAN OR BOETHUS.
KAKAN OR KEECHOS.
BINNUTER OR BINOTHRIS. Female succession permitted by law
UTNAS OR TLAS.
SENTA OR SETHENES.
NEFERKA-RA OR NEPHERCHE-RES.

IIIrd DYNASTY OF MEMPHIS.
NEB-KA, SER, TOTA, MESOCHRIS, SOUPHIS, TOSERTASIS, ACHES, SEPHURIS, KERPHERES.

IVth DYN. OF MEMPHIS.
SORIS.
KHUFU OR CHEOPS. Erected the great pyramid at Gizeh.
RATATF OR RATOISES.
SHAFRA.
MENKAURA OR MYCERINUS. Built the Third Pyramid.

Vth DYN. OF MEMPHIS.
USERKAF, SAHURA, NEFERKA-RA, RANUSER, MEN-KAU-HOR, TATKARA, UNAS.

VIth DYN. OF ELEPHANTINE.
TETA. PEPI. MERENRA, son. NEFERKARA, son. NITOCRIS.

EARLY CIV

DATE FOR ACCESSION OF M
G. Wilkinson - - 2691 B.C.
Stuart Poole - - 2717 B.C.
Bunsen (later view) 3059 B.C.
Bunsen (early view) 3623 B.C.

CAUSES OF THIS

The Egyptians "did not enter into any chronological idea", "save in a new least almost non-existent." This is the uni Rawlinson.

"Chronology cannot be elicited from their "The greatest obstacle to the establish circumstance that the Egyptians then MANETHO, the Egyptian Historian, w divided Egyptian history into three peri MANETHO, the Old Empire, the Middle and the New Empire, to which he assi dynasties—thirty-one in all—b All Egyptologers but one—M. Mariette or less extent, contemporary, and the to the extent to which contemporary

EGYPT'S THREE EMPIRES
1. "OLD EMPIRE" (Native Dynasties) 2450
2. "MIDDLE EMPIRE" (the Hyksos or Shep
3. "NEW EMPIRE" (Native Dynasties), 150

SHIN-NONG. 146. He teaches the art of Husbandry, the method of making Bread from Wheat, Wine from Rice, &c. Perhaps the Shem of the Bible.

2155 B.C. Eclipse of the sun observed by the Chinese astronomers, according to DU HALDE.
2000 ? Worship of Brahma in India. The Sanskrit, or sacred language used. The Vedas (four) and Puranas written (?). The Vedas are respectively entitled the YAJUR, RIG, SAMA, and ATHARVA, and are known only to a few learned persons of the "higher castes". The "PURANAS" are quite generally known, and exercise an extensive and practical influence on Hindoo Society. They are of a legendary nature, with fantastic theories of creation, destruction, and renovation of worlds, religious doctrines, rites, &c.

1998

1852

2200 BC **2100 BC** **2000 BC** **1900 BC**

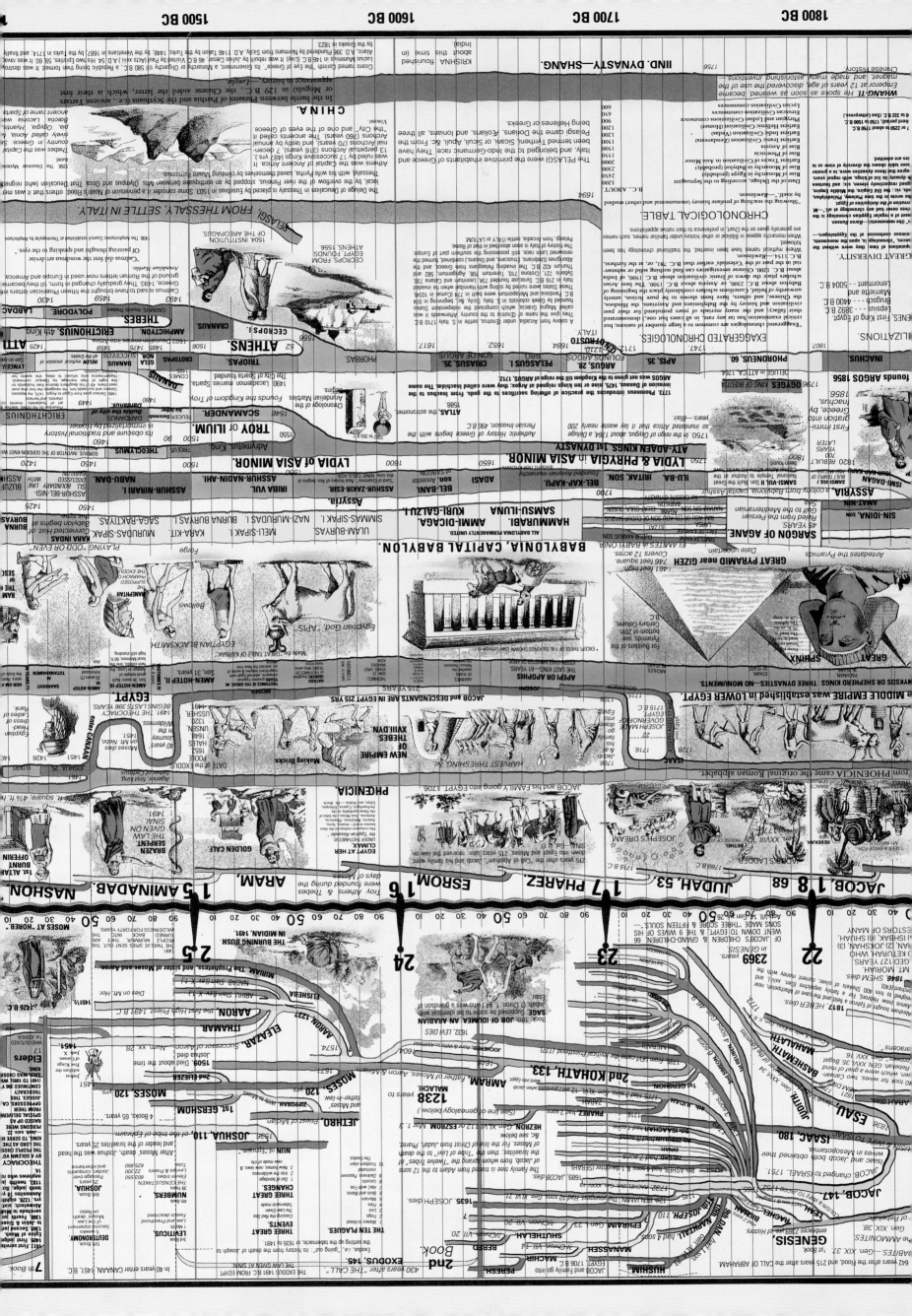

The Moabite Stone

Dating from the 9th Century BC, the Moabite stone is one of the oldest complete specimens of alphabetic writing known to scholars. Apart from a few fragmentary inscriptions, no other Moabite literature has survived and the stone is remarkable in that it contains every letter, bar one, of the ancient alphabet.

Mesha, King of Moab at the time of Ahab, set up this memorial pillar in his important native city of Dibon, just north of the Arnon. A black basalt stone, just over a metre high, it was discovered intact in AD 1868. Unfortunately, the local people, hoping to realise a higher renumeration from a number of vendors, broke the stone into several pieces. Luckily a cast of the intact stone was taken prior to this act of vandalism and in 1873 the Moabite stone was taken to the Louvre and there restored.

The thirty-five lines of text are similar to contemporary Hebrew inscriptions and provide additional information about the Biblical reference to King Omin in Kings 1, chapter XVI.

The Moabite Stone

900 BC

Built by Mesha, King of Moab

Black basalt

Size: over a metre high

Discovered: AD 1868

Taken to the Louvre, Paris, in 1873

Inscription in Ancient Phoenician

The Rosetta Stone

The Rosetta Stone was discovered in 1799 by a Frenchman during repairs to a fort on the Nile Delta. Its importance lies in the fact that it bears inscriptions in two languages and three scripts (hieroglyphics, demotic and Greek) and so for the first time enabled Egyptian hieroglyphics to be deciphered. Even with the help of the Rosetta stone, unravelling the puzzle to create a basis for future translation was a task which took Egyptologists over twenty years to complete.

The stone itself is nearly four feet high and just over two feet wide. Upon its irregular black basalt face is recorded commemorative information to mark the accession of Ptolemy V Epiphanes to the Egyptian throne in 197-196 BC; this commemoration was apparently written by the priests of Memphis.

The Rosetta Stone

195 BC

Written by Memphis priests

Marked accession of Ptolemy V Epiphanes to throne

197-196 BC

Black basalt

Size: About 4 feet high and 2 feet wide

Discovered on Nile Delta: AD 1799

Now in the British Museum, London

Inscriptions in 2 languages and 3 scripts (hieroglyphics, demotic and Greek)

Babylonian brick

This set of bricks from ancient Chaldæa in Mesopotamia bears a cuneiform inscription. Until the 19th century knowledge of Babylonia was scant but discovery of monuments and tablets and decipherment of cuneiform script revealed far more about a civilization that spanned 3,000 years.

Megaliths and standing stones

With the development of agriculture, communities became more stable and rural centres emerged. These provided not only homes but the springboard for cultural development, including religion and ritual. In the first place burial of the dead and associated rites gave rise to long barrows and megalithic tombs. By 3200 BC single standing stones (menhirs), rows of stones and stone circles, along with circular ditched enclosures (henges), had appeared right across north-western Europe. Britain alone has the remains of about a thousand stone circles, the most famous of which is undoubtedly Stonehenge on Salisbury Plain which superseded Avebury as the ritual centre of southern England.

Facts about Stonehenge

Built in three main stages from about 2100 to 1400 BC

Each Sarsen block weighs approximately 26 tons

An estimated 1000 men would have been needed to haul each of the great stones from Marlborough Downs

The bluestones used for the stone circle (1550 BC) came from the Preseli hills in South Wales, some 320 kilometres (200 miles) away

The diameter of the overall area is about 100 metres (320 feet)

Its axis is aligned to the position of the sunrise at the summer solstice

The erection of the third phase of Stonehenge (with the sarsen circle and trilithons) probably took 2,000,000 hours of hard labour

Traditionally it was thought that the altar stone may have been used for human sacrifice. There is no real evidence to support this but ritual burials have been discovered there

---

Noah and the Flood

According to the Bible, before the onset of the Great Deluge, on God's instruction Noah built an ark to precise measurements. He proceeded to take on board and thereby rescue his family and one pair of each species of animal. Torrential rain made the waters rise for one hundred and fifty days. When the deluge of water finally began to recede, Noah sent forth a raven and then two doves before one bird returned with an olive leaf, thus establishing the existence of land. In all, it was seven months before the ark came to rest again on the mountains of Ararat and at last the animals could be released.

17th century theories

Sir Walter Raleigh, imprisoned in the Tower of London from 1603 to 1616, spent some part of this thirteen-year captivity in writing a five-volume *History of the World*. In this he proposed that only the animals of the Old World could have been included in the ark and that therefore all the creatures of the New World must have evolved from those of the Old.

In 1685 Matthew Hale, Lord Chief Justice of England, propounded that as only a few of all the known species could have fitted into the ark these must have been the original ancestors of all other species existing since.

Archaeological evidence

In Mesopotamia, at Ur, Kish, Nineveh, Erech and Shuruppak, excavations have revealed flood layers and deep deposits of water-laid clay, mud and sand dating from various times between 4000 to 2000 BC. It would seem there were several cataclysmic floods, probably due to the rising of the Tigris and the Euphrates, augmented by torrential rainfall and possibly a tidal bore.

Alphabets and script

It is interesting to note that the earliest scripts and writing consisted of numbers only, and were for recording business accounts in about 3500 BC in Mesopotamia. It was there too that people first began to inscribe in wet cakes of clay with hollow reed stems; many of these clay tablets have survived and provide much interesting information about the past. The word cuneiform means 'wedge-shaped'. Derived from the shape of the reed stylus, it is used to describe the ancient inscriptions of Persia and Assyria. Gradually stylized drawings became pictographs, each one representing a syllable.

Egyptian hieroglyphics were unique, examples on papyrus (paper made from flattened reeds) appearing from about 2600 BC while further East, Chinese script developed quite independently of any Mesopotamian origins — as did the Mayan scripts in the West.

The earliest alphabet appeared in Syria in about 1400 BC and used thirty signs. North Semitic writing represented only consonants and it was the Greeks who invented the alphabet, as we know it, with symbols for vowels too. Today the Chinese alphabet has 60,000 characters.

Today's meaning	Picto-graphic from 3000 BC	Early cuneiform about 2400 BC	Late Assyrian about 650 BC	Sumerian phonetic meaning
barley				še
cow				áb
day				ud
orchard				kiri₆
water				a

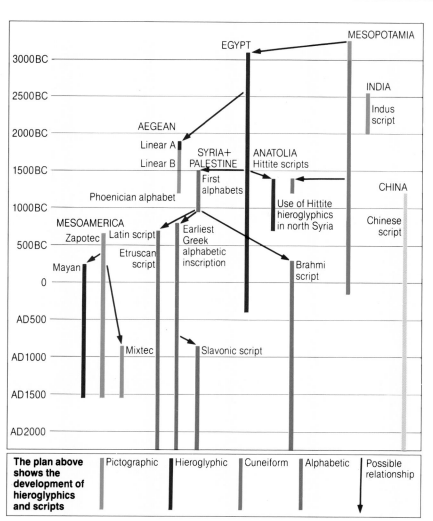

3000BC	EGYPT		MESOPOTAMIA	
2500BC			INDIA	
			Indus script	
2000BC	AEGEAN			
1500BC	Linear A / Linear B	SYRIA+ PALESTINE	ANATOLIA Hittite scripts	
		First alphabets		
1000BC	Phoenician alphabet		Use of Hittite hieroglyphics in north Syria	CHINA
500BC	MESOAMERICA Zapotec / Latin script	Earliest Greek alphabetic inscription		Chinese script
	Mayan / Etruscan script		Brahmi script	
0				
AD500				
AD1000	Mixtec	Slavonic script		
AD1500				
AD2000				

The plan above shows the development of hieroglyphics and scripts — Pictographic | Hieroglyphic | Cuneiform | Alphabetic | Possible relationship

The Minoans

The Minoans were a Bronze Age civilization of enormous wealth, sophistication and influence. From the island of Crete, where their kings ruled in splendid palaces — the most famous being Knossos — a well organized economy exported woollen textiles, weapons, finely decorated pottery, timber, and stone bowls. In 1450 BC a catastrophic volcanic eruption on the nearby island of Thera (now Santorin) and its attendant tidal wave were followed by a further earthquake. The effects of this, combined with the incursions of opportunist Greek invaders, finally brought to an end over a thousand years of fine civilization and domination of the Mediterranean world.

Ancient cities

The Ruins of Nineveh

Nineveh, the oldest city in Assyria, was set on the fertile west bank of the Tigris and 2,500 years ago, during the reign of Sennacherib, developed into a splendid walled city with fifteen enormous gates, fine streets and squares and an elaborate canal system. Most magnificent of all was Sennacherib's palace — over six hundred feet square with eighty rooms and a grand entrance flanked by colossal stone human-headed bulls, twenty feet high and twenty feet long. In all, ten bulls stood guard by the main doorways.

Following earlier intermittent excavations, it was Sir Henry Layard who discovered the stone bulls in 1849 and took back with him to England an incredible collection of bas reliefs and inscribed tablets uncovered from the great library of Ashurbanipal II, a successor to Sennacherib.

Ashurbanipal had ordered his scribes to collect and copy ancient texts and over 20,000 tablets and fragments of tablets formed the 'K' collection, an invaluable store of information about the administration, religion, mathematics, science and literature of ancient Mesopotamia.

Nineveh
Oldest city in Assyria
On the west bank of the Tigris
2,500 years old
Built during the reign of Sennacherib
Sennacherib's palace: over 600 feet square with 80 rooms. Grand entrance houses ten 20-foot high stone human-headed bulls
Discovered by Sir Henry Layard in AD 1849
The great library housed a vast collection of inscribed tablets
The collection of over 20,000 tablets and fragments of tablets formed the invaluable 'K' collection from ancient Mesopotamia

Babylon

The capital of ancient Babylonia, set on the left bank of the Euphrates, the site of Babylon is in present-day Iraq. A religious centre, it was a place of power and importance but achieved its greatest fame in the reign of Nebuchadnezzar, especially for its ziggurat or temple tower.

Greek writer Herodotus described Babylon as standing on a broad plain and forming an exact square laid out as a rectangular grid, with moat, ditch, embankment and towers, streets and houses. Certainly his description of the ziggurat appears authentic: '...when one is about halfway up, one finds a resting-place and seats, where persons are wont to sit some time on the way to the summit.'

Excavations at the turn of the century revealed double inner and outer walls on the left bank of the river, the great Ishtar gate nearly forty feet high, brick-paved streets the sides of which were decorated with brick lions, dragons and bulls, spacious temples and a palace area covering some thirteen acres.

Babylon
Capital of ancient Babylonia
Set on left bank of the Euphrates (in present-day Iraq)
Achieved its greatest fame in the reign of Nebuchadnezzar
Renowned for its ziggurat or temple tower and hanging gardens

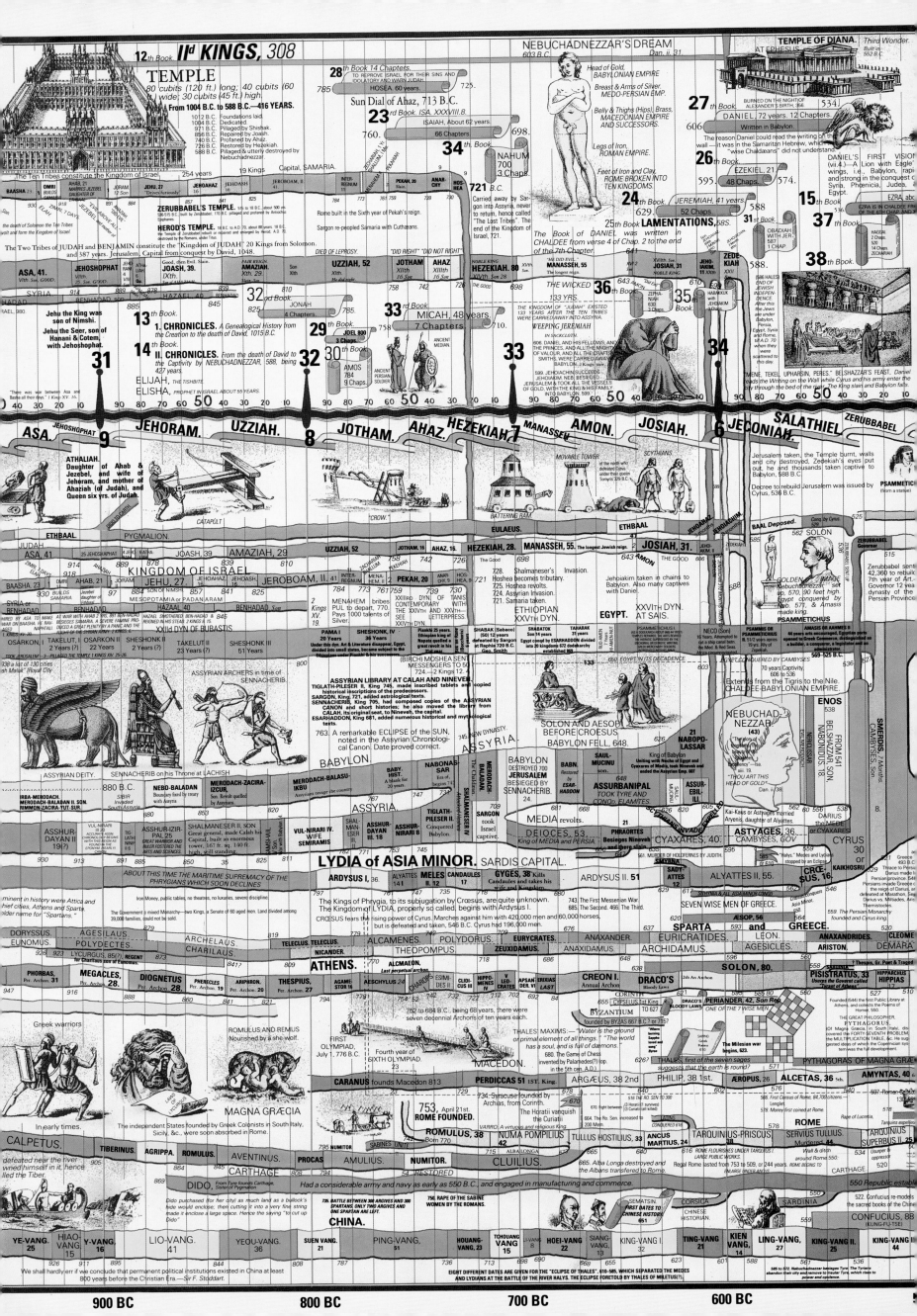

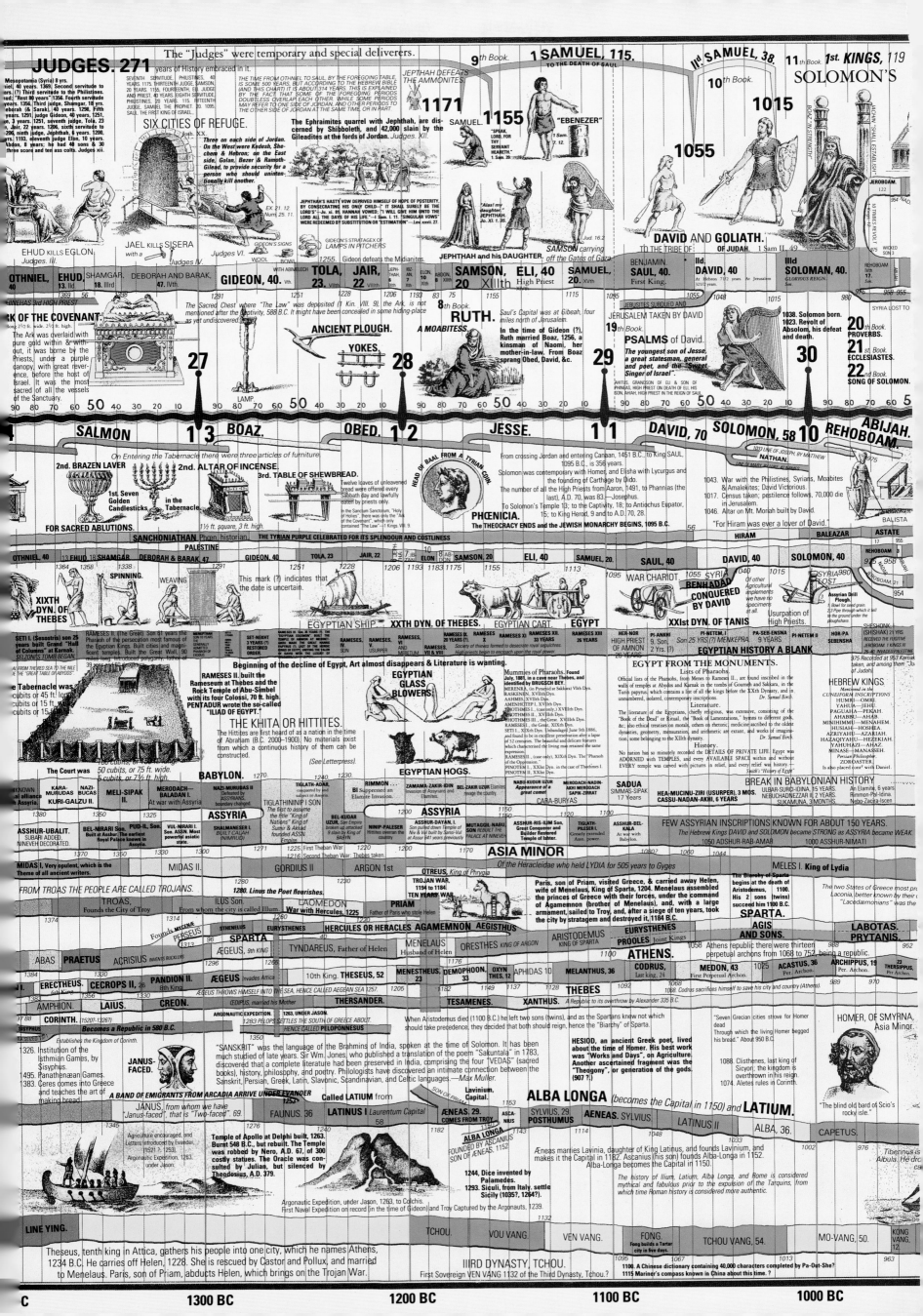

Thebes

Thebes is in fact the Greek name for the ancient city of Niut-Ammon in Upper Egypt. Probably founded under the First Dynasty, this was the centre for the worship of Ammon and was in 1600 BC the Egyptian capital under the New Kingdom. Its temple ruins survive near the villages of Karnac and Luxor in Egypt today.

Ancient Thebes was about six miles square. The city of the living and the royal temples were built on the eastern bank while the necropolis, mortuary temples and homes of the priests and their supporting 'staff' were to be found on the western side of the Nile.

A city which reflects the richness of the ancient Egyptian Empire when it was in it heyday, Thebes once housed in splendour many of the most famous Egyptian archeological remains — the Colossi of Memnon, The temples of Karnac and Luxor, the Valley of the Kings (Tutankhamen's is just one of sixty tombs there) and the temples of Rameses II and Rameses III. The three-tiered temple of Hatshepsut is set in the bay of cliffs and approached through an avenue of sphinxes.

Thebes	
Thebes is its Greek name	
The ancient city was called Niut-Ammon	
The site is in Upper Egypt	
Probably founded under the First Dynasty	
Centre for worship of Ammon	
In 1600 BC was the Egyptian capital under the New Kingdom	
Ancient Thebes was about 6 miles square	
Site of the Colossi of Memnon, the temples of Karnac and Luxor, the valley of the Tombs of the Kings and the temples of Rameses II and Rameses III	

Tyre

Tyre was a seaport of ancient Phoenicia, built on a peninsula, once an island, in what is now Lebanon. Of the two harbours, there are remains of the one in the north but the southern harbour has filled with sand.

Tyre was originally founded as a colony of Sidon. It became subject to Egypt in the fifteenth century BC, but was never under the control of Israel.

Hiram, the King of Tyre, was in fact friendly with David and Solomon — he even supplied them with building materials for Jerusalem. Ahab's queen, Jezebel, was the daughter of a king of Tyre and Sidon.

The city escaped the plundering of the coastal towns by Sennacherib but succumbed to Ashurbanipal in 669 BC and was besieged by Nebuchadrezzar II, finally submitting to him after a thirteen-year siege. The city was a centre for trade in the Mediterranean.

Tyre
Originally founded as a colony of Sidon
Subject to Egypt in the 15th century BC
Hiram, king of Tyre, was friendly with David and Solomon and supplied them with building materials for Jerusalem
Ahab's queen, Jezebel, was the daughter of a king of Tyre and Sidon
The city succumbed to Ashurbanipal in 669 BC
Tyre submitted to Nebuchadrezzar II after 13 years of siege

The Shang Dynasty in China		
Origins: in north-east China 3000 BC	Developed: 1800 BC	Collapsed: 11th century BC
Established Chinese cultural traditions and formed the basis of their civilization		
Sacrificial pits in splendid royal tombs held many bodies of humans, dogs and horses		
Oracle bones (bovine shoulder blades or tortoise shells) were used to divine the future		
The Shang kings moved to new capitals six times, including Cheng-chou and An-yang		
The Shang royal family delegated power rather like the later European feudal system		
Skilled bronze technology and culture was most developed along the Yellow River		
Astrologers developed a calendar with 30 days to a month and 360 days to a year		

Sidon

Sidon was the main city of Phoenicia founded in the third millennium BC. Mentioned by Homer and in the Old Testament, it was a prosperous thriving city but, because it is buried under the modern town, it has not been excavated properly and so its history remains somewhat obscure.

However, a large necropolis and numerous sarchophagi and pieces of jewellery have been uncovered nearby.

The ancient city's sea mole and wall can still be located as well as the twin harbours.

Greek and Roman gods

The gods and goddesses depicted in the timeflow chart have been referred to by their Roman names as opposed to their Greek titles. In fact the Romans absorbed a good deal of the Greek civilization — such as their religion and architecture — proceeding to adapt it into and blend it with their own way of life. They then took this knowledge with them as their empire extended, so spreading a cultural heritage that had an impact on most of the known western world, including its language. Quite a few of the words we use today are derived from the names of these gods.

Juno, Queen of Heaven

Jupiter, father of the gods

Neptune, brother of Jupiter

Vulcan, son of Juno

Greek name	Roman name	areas of responsibility
Hera	Juno	womanhood: marriage, motherhood and babies; the queen of heaven
Zeus	Jupiter	father of gods and men; the sky-deity; justice, virtue and the law
Poseidon	Neptune	earthquakes and water; the sea
Hephaestus	Vulcan	fire and furnace; patron of smiths and craftsmen
Artemis	Diana	the moon; chastity
Aphrodite	Venus	love and fertility; beauty
Ares	Mars	war; agriculture, flocks and herds
Hermes	Mercury	message carrying; conducting the dead to Hades; trade
Athena	Minerva	war; wisdom; arts and crafts
Morpheus	Morpheus	dreams
Nemesis	Nemesis	retribution
Demeter	Ceres	corn
Dionysus	Bacchus	wine; inspiration and ecstasy; fertility
Hypnos	Somnus	sleep
Irene	Pax	peace
Nike	Victoria	victory
Pan	Sylvanus	flocks and herds
Kronus	Saturn	sowing of corn; agriculture

Power and influence

Egypt: crafts and agriculture

Egypt was a land rich in natural resources. Its rich alluvium supported many crops, providing pasture for cattle, sheep, goats and pigs, while fish and fowl abounded in the Nile and its overflow. Papyrus reeds proved a marvellous source of material — for papermaking, basketware, boat building and matting, with the fine mud in the river banks an excellent source of potters' clay. There was limestone and sandstone for the mason; alabaster, copper ore and gold for the craftsmen; while the fertile Nile Valley encouraged the cultivation of wheat and barley, flax and cotton. Orchards of fig, date and palm were irrigated by water channels.

Grapes were grown in oases and delta areas — in vineyards that were under royal or temple ownership, or sometimes private concerns.

Generally, this was a rich land — one that could support highly skilled artisans, scribes, priests and a prosperous trade with other countries. However, agriculture was dependent upon the annual flooding of the Nile

Egyptians spinning

to create fertile silt and there were occasions when this was repeatedly too low, resulting in famine. Irrigation methods such as the shaduf were developed to maintain the crops of grain during their short growing period. Flax, and later cotton, was woven to make clothes and linen sheets which were stored in great chests or in hampers made from palm fibre.

Making bricks in Ancient Egypt

Houses were built of mud bricks with walls and floors that were sometimes plastered and, in richer homes, decorated with murals. Towns were evidently bustling and overcrowded.

Royal patrons gave great impetus to the arts and this led to the creation of musical instruments, light chariots, exquisite jewellery, amulets, inlaid cabinets, polychrome glass and faïence vases, sculptures and frescoes.

Much of what we know about rural and urban life has been readily understood through the vivid paintings and beautiful artefacts preserved in the arid Egyptian sands for thousands of years — often in burial tombs where the way of life was depicted to surround the soul and accompany it on its journey to the afterlife.

Making glass vessels

Beyond the Bronze Age: weapons and armoury

The bow and arrow is the oldest of projectile weapons, used since Paleolithic times. It can be seen in stone carvings of Egyptian pharaohs and Assyrian kings but was not greatly used by the Romans. (Crossbows were not used until about 300 BC, in China.)

Sumerian spearmen grouped together to make a protective wall of shields.

Greek soldier

Roman legionary

Assyrian archers

1000 BC: The Assyrians dominated the Near East through aggressive warfare — undertaken by infantry, heavily armed lancers, cavalry (both riders and horses were protected by armour), charioteers, shield bearers and archers. They dug tunnels and used battering rams and scaling ladders to attack besieged cities.

Greek soldiers wore body armour and helmets made of bronze and carried large circular or kidney-shaped shields.

The cuirass, or body armour, was originally made of leather. Usually it

consisted of a back and breastplate buckled together but sometimes a breastplate was used alone.

Roman legionaries wore round iron helmets and a cuirass made of metal or leather hoops around the body. They carried long rectangular shields which curved protectively around the body.

Scale armour and chainmail was developed in Roman times. Chainmail made in western Europe was usually riveted. Oriental mail was generally made of butted rings.

Roman armies developed many specialized pieces of machinery to enable them to besiege enemy cities. Catapults hurled rocks or flaming darts over walls and ramparts; siege towers (covered in skins to protect them from fire), scaling ladders and ramps helped them gain access to the city while battering rams attacked the walls. The soldiers carried their shields over their heads to create a shell of armour called a 'testudo' or tortoise.

Catapults projected rocks or flaming darts

The crow, a huge grappling iron

Balista to hurl rocks

Battering ram to attack walls

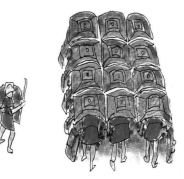

A protective testudo of shields

End of the 39 BOOKS of the O.T. 397 B.C. and 3607 A.M.

380. ALEXANDER TRANSFERS THE SEAT OF GOVERNMENT FROM MACEDONIA TO SUSA, IN BABYLON.

(Dan. vii. 5) SECOND BEAST A Bear with three ribs in its mouth, that is, Medo-Persia, with Babylon, Egypt, and Lydia.

DANIEL VIII.5.—"Behold an he goat came from the west on the face of the whole earth, and touched not the ground, & had a notable horn between his eyes."

RAM WITH TWO HORNS.

And he smote the ram and brake his two horns. Dan. viii.7

39th Book

MALACHI 420 to 397 23 Yrs 4 Chaps.

554. Daniel cast into the Lion's den.

16th Book. NEH 13 CHAPS. 445 12 433

And the goat waxed very great.

THE PHAROS OF ALEXANDRIA. Seventh Wonder. BY PTOLEMY-PHILADELPHUS 280 B.C. 550 feet high.

ROMAN GOVERNMENT.

753 B.C. TO A.D. 476—1229 YEARS.

- B.C. 753. ROME FOUNDED by Romulus (VARRO). (Other dates: Flaccus, 752; Cato, 751; Polybius, 750; Fabius Pictor, 747; Cincius, 728 B.C.)
- B.C. 509. KINGDOM ENDED. REPUBLIC BEGAN, Consuls (yearly).
- B.C. 501. FIRST DICTATOR, Titus Lartius.
- B.C. 494. TRIBUNES of PLEBEIANS appointed.
- B.C. 484. QUÆSTORS appointed (about).
- B.C. 458. CINCINNATUS DICTATOR.
- B.C. 451. DECEMVIRI created; Laws of Twelve Tables.
- B.C. 449. DECEMVIRI abolished.
- B.C. 444. MILITARY TRIBUNES first appointed, with consular power.
- B.C. 443. Office of CENSOR created.
- B.C. 409. PLEBEIAN QUÆSTORS (Three) first chosen.
- B.C. 366. PLEBEIAN CONSUL first chosen (Lucius Sextus).
- B.C. 60. FIRST TRIUMVIRATE—JULIUS CÆSAR, CRASSUS, & POMPEY.
- B.C. 53. CRASSUS killed by PARTHIANS.
- B.C. 50. CIVIL WAR between CÆSAR and POMPEY. End of FIRST TRIUMVIRATE.
- B.C. 48. CÆSAR defeated POMPEY at PHARSALIA.
- B.C. 46. CÆSAR DICTATOR for ten years.
- B.C. 44. CÆSAR KILLED in the Senate House.
- B.C. 43. SECOND TRIUMVIRATE—OCTAVIUS, LEPIDUS, & ANTONY.
- B.C. 36. LEPIDUS expelled from the TRIUMVIRATE.
- B.C. 31. OCTAVIUS defeated ANTONY at Actium.
- B.C. 30. OCTAVIUS VIRTUAL EMPEROR.
- B.C. 27. OCTAVIUS proclaimed EMPEROR as AUGUSTUS CÆSAR.
- A.D. 364. EMPIRE first divided into Eastern and Western.
- A.D. 476. EMPIRE ended—"FALL OF ROME."

FOURTH BEAST WITH TEN HORNS. Dan. vii. 7.

SIXTH WONDER, 302-290 B.C. THE BRASS COLOSSUS OF RHODES Was 105 ft. high. Built 290 B.C. Fell, by an earthquake, 224 B.C. Was sold by the Sixth Caliph to a Jew, who loaded 900 Camels with 800 lbs. each (360 tons), about A.D. 623.

FOURTH WONDER. At Olympia, 433 B.C. Of Gold and Ivory. By Phidias. JUPITER OLYMPIÆ

MAUSOLEUM, Fifth Wonder, at Halicarnassus, 350 B.C.

DIOGENES AND HIS TUB. The Cynic Philosopher of Athens.

END OF THE O.T. 397 B.C.

ALEXANDRIAN LIBRARY. 284 B.C., by Ptolemy-Philadelphus, 700,000 Volumes. Partly burned by Julius Cæsar, 47 B.C. Burned by Omar, A.D. 640.

AHASHUERUS, XERXES, or ARTAXERXES-LONGIMANUS and QUEEN ESTHER.

CLEOPATRA'S

HEBREW DRESS.

36 **37** **38** **39**

90 80 70 **50** 40 30 20 10 90 80 70 60 **50** 40 30 20 10 90 80 70 60 **50** 40 30 20 10 90 80 70 60 **50**

ABIUD. ELIAKIM. AZOR. SADOC. ACHIM. ELIUD. ELEAZAR. MATTHAN. JACOB.

307. SCYTHIANS INVADE CALEDONIA

CALEDONIA SCOTLAND

4 **3** **2** **1**

SOCRATES drinking the hemlock, 399.

ARCHIMEDES SCREW AND LEVER, Of Syracuse, in Sicily.

CLEPSYDRA, or Water-Clock, at Rome, 158 B.C., by Scipio Nasica. Alfred measured time by wax tapers.

BRITAIN.

PLATO.

DEMOSTHENES.

PALESTINE or JUDÆA.

APOCHRYPHAL HISTORY ENDS, 135

PERSIAN EMPIRE, 559 to 330, 229 yrs.

BABYLON 15 miles square. Walls 350 ft. high. Walls 87 ft. thick. 25 Brass Gates on each side.

ALEXANDER THE GREAT.

DARIUS III. or CODOMANUS, 6.

PERSIAN EMPIRE.

MACEDONIAN EMPIRE, ALEXANDER III.

XERXES ARTAXERXES. I. LONGIMANUS, 40. DARIUS II. NOTHUS ARTAXERXES II. MNEMON, ARTAXERXES. III. OCHUS.

EGYPT under the 13 PTOLEMIES, 323 to 30 B.C. 293 years.

PTOLEMY I. LAGUS, 38. PTOLEMY II. PHILADELPHUS. PTOLEMY III. EUERGETES. PTOLEMY IV. PHILOPATOR PTOLEMY V. EPIPHANES PTOLEMY VI. PHILOMETOR 35. PTOLEMY VII. PHYSCON 29 CLEOPATRA

SYRIA under the SALEUCIDÆ, 247 years 312 to 65.

SELEUCUS I. ANTIOCHUS I. ANTIOCHUS II. SELEUCUS II. ANTIOCHUS III. SELEUCUS IV ANTIOCHUS VIII.

CAPPADOCIA ASIA MINOR.

ARIARATHES I. ARIARATHES II. ARIARATHES III. ARIARATHES IV. ARIARATHES V. ARIARATHES VI.

PONTUS.

MITHRIDATES II. MITHRIDATES III. MITHRIDATES IV. PHARNACES I. MITHRIDATES V. MITHRIDATES VI. 60.

BITHYNIA.

ZIPÆTAS 37 NICOMEDES Ist. PRUSIAS Ist. PRUSIAS 2nd NICOMEDES 2nd. 58.

PERGAMUS.

PHILETÆRUS EUMENES Ist. ATTALUS Ist. EUMENES II. ATTALUS II.

HERODOTUS FATHER OF HISTORY

HERODOTUS XENOPHON ÆSCHINES DEMOSTHENES, 60.

SPARTA.

ATHENS. ANNUAL ARCHONS.

THEMISTOCLES PERICLES

SPARTA AGIS. SPARTA joins the League.

CASSANDER 25 THEBES ACHÆAN LEAGUE REVIVED ATHENS.

THRACE EPIRUS. PYRRHUS Greece a Roman province.

LYSIMACHUS MACEDON.

PHILIP ARIDÆUS ANTIGONUS-BONATUS PHILIP V. PERSEUS.

PARTHENON OF ATHENS. TO MINERVA.

SYRACUSE, SICILY.

ROMAN REPUBLIC.

CHINESE WALL. BY CHIHOANG-TI.

MITHRIDATES "The Great," Wise and Virtuous.

PARTHIA. ARSACES TIRIDATES 33.

CARTHAGE.

HAMILCAR. HANNIBAL 37.

SYLLA B.C. 107. Quaestor. B.C. 88. Consul. B.C. 82. Dictator. 28.

J. CÆSAR. CRASSUS. POMPEY. CICERO, 63 ORATOR & PHILOSR. VIRGIL, 51.

TCHING-TING-VANG. GUCI-TIE-VANG. NGAN-VANG. LIE-VANG. HIEN-VANG. NGAN-VANG, II. TCHOU-KUM. CHI-HOANG-TI KAO-SOU HOEI-TI VEN-TI. VOU-TI 53. TCHAO-TI. SUEN-TI.

IVTH DYN.—TSIN. VTH DYN-HAN.

400 BC   **300 BC**   **200 BC**   **100 BC**

Pioneers of new ideals

The Greeks

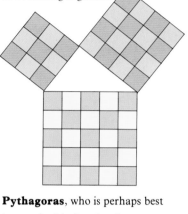

Plato (427-348 BC) was a great philosopher, many of whose doctrines have influenced human thought ever since he formulated them in his Dialogues over 2000 years ago. His central conception was of a world where ideas alone are real and permanent and material objects imperfect and ephemeral. As well as immortality and substance, he examined justice and morality, truth, rhetoric, form and beauty, law and ethics, religion and education. The word 'platonic' derives from his discourse on love and affection free from sensual desire.

Hippocrates, born on the island of Kos, is known as 'the father of medicine'. A renowned doctor who developed structured diagnosis of illness, the ideals he proposed are encapsulated in the Hippocratic oath, for centuries regarded as the correct rules of conduct for doctors to follow — so much so that medical students have continued to use the oath when graduating from universities and medical schools.

The first Olympic Games took place in 776 BC at Olympia; they continued to be held every fourth year until AD 393. At first a single event, which took the form of a race the length of the stadium, the Games soon developed to include discus throwing, wrestling, the pentathlon, javelin and the broad jump. Skill, courage, sportsmanship and gracefulness were considered as important as victory.

Homer in 750 BC wrote the epic narrative poems, the *Iliad* and the *Odyssey*, still considered two of the greatest works in world literature.

Thales: philosopher, mathematician, astronomer and statesman. Credited with having introduced geometry into Greece, he developed several theorems regarding lines, circles and angles and also suggested that water was the principle and origin of all material things. Thales believed the universe to be a living organism.

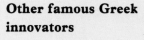

Pythagoras, who is perhaps best known for his theories about geometry and arithmetic, was also one of the first to express the belief that the earth and the universe were spherical and to propose the idea that the explanation of the universe lay in numbers.

Aesop, a slave from Thrace who was granted his freedom by his master, is reputed to have written a collection of moral tales about animals. The values expressed in these may have been derived in part from a medieval compilation of the stories.

Other famous Greek innovators

Literature and drama
Euripedes 480-406 BC: author of great Attic tragedies
Sophocles: an Athenian tragic poet
Aeschylus: founded Greek tragic drama
Sappho 610-580 BC: A fine and influential lyric poetess from Lesbos; legends claim she committed suicide by throwing herself from a high cliff into the sea because her love for the boatman Phaon was unrequited.

Mathematics and astronomy
Archimedes: mechanical inventor and mathemetician from Syracuse; invented the Archimedes screw and the principle of displacement of water.

Aristotle: a pupil of Plato, he invented logic and wrote works on zoology, politics, and metaphysics, philosophy, democracy and law.

Diogenes: 412 BC philosopher and cynic from Athens who was supposed to have resided in an earthenware jar. According to Seneca, he was fit only to live in a barrel! Perhaps this comment gave rise to the idea.

Socrates 469-399 BC: philosopher whose death sentence was to drink hemlock.
Democritus: advanced the theory that the world was formed by the concourse of atoms.

History
Herodotus: 5th century BC; author, geographer and traveller; the first true European historian.

Confucius

Born in the state of Lu in China in about 551 BC, Confucius was an obscure teacher who became one of the most influential men in world history; his ideas greatly influenced the development of civilization throughout eastern Asia.

Self-educated and probably from impoverished nobility, he eventually became one of the most learned men of his time. His main intent was the relief of suffering. Deeply concerned with the problems of poverty, oppression, crippling taxation and war, he hoped to attain a position in administration from which he could put into practice his ideas about the reform of government.

Unquestionably he presented a threat to his rulers and when no position of real authority proved forthcoming he began to teach instead, gathering disciples around him and eventually procuring posts for them. Disillusioned by the ineffectiveness of this and of his own role, in his fifties Confucius set off on a long and dangerous journey through different states of China, trying to find a ruler who would put his revolutionary theories into operation. It was not until he was sixty-seven that he returned again to Lu where he continued to teach until his death, five years later.

Confucius was not authoritarian or dogmatic. He believed in individual choice and the right of people to make decisions for themselves. He advocated an empirical approach:
To hear much, select what is good and follow it; to see much and take careful note of it; these are the steps by which one ascends to understanding.

His teachings about the equality and fellowship of man were largely responsible for the demise of an authoritative aristocracy in China.

He believed the right to govern depended upon the ability to make those one governed happy.

He believed in the importance of some level of education for all — to create the opportunity for ability to flourish. He saw war as an evil but one sometimes necessary to secure justice — when it should be pursued vigorously by armies well-informed of the reasons for their actions.

A truly virtuous man, he said, desiring to be established himself, seeks to establish others; desiring success, he seeks to help others to succeed.

Confucianism has influenced Chinese thinking and far eastern culture more deeply than any other doctrine.

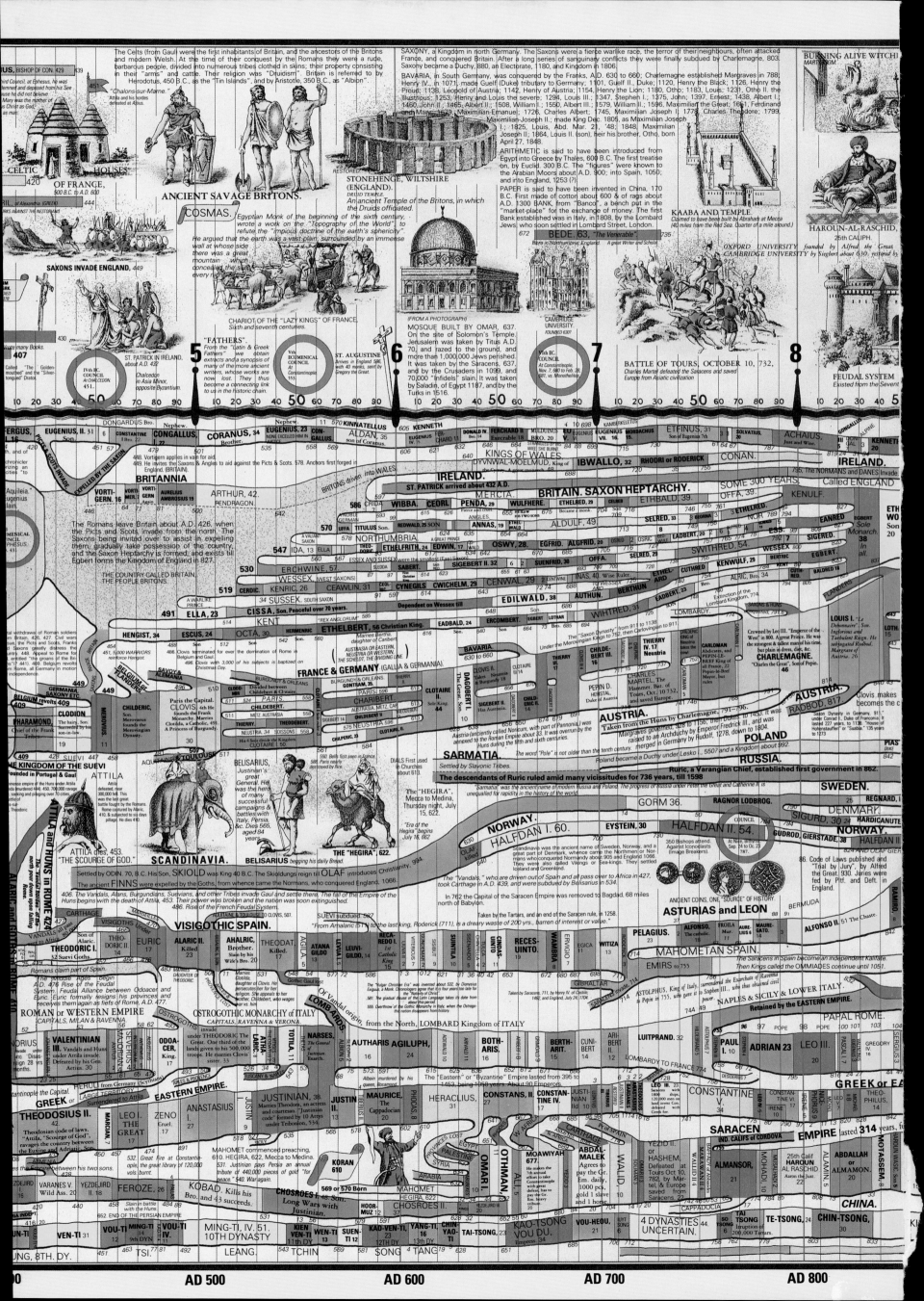

The Celts (from Gaul) were the first inhabitants of Britain, and the ancestors of the Britons and modern Welsh. At the time of their conquest by the Romans they were a rude, barbarous people, divided into numerous tribes clothed in skins; their property consisting in their "arms" and cattle. Their religion was "Druidism". Britain is referred to by Herodotus, 450 B.C., as the "Tin Islands", and by Aristotle, 350 B.C., as "Albion."

SAXONY, a Kingdom in north Germany. The Saxons were a fierce warlike race, the terror of their neighbours, often attacked France, and conquered Britain. After a long series of sanguinary conflicts they were finally subdued by Charlemagne, 803. Saxony became a Duchy, 880, an Electorate, 1180, and Kingdom in 1806.

BAVARIA, in South Germany, was conquered by the Franks, A.D. 630 to 660; Charlemagne established Margraves in 788; Henry IV., in 1071, made Guelf (Duke) tributary to Germany; 1101, Guelf II., Duke; 1120, Henry the Black; 1126, Henry the Proud; 1138, Leopold of Austria; 1142, Henry of Austria; 1154, Henry the Lion; 1180, Otho; 1183, Louis; 1231, Otho II. the Illustrious; 1253, Henry and Louis the severe; 1294, Louis III.; 1347, Stephen I.; 1375, John; 1397, Ernest; 1438, Albert I.; 1460, John II.; 1465, Albert II.; 1508, William I.; 1550, Albert II.; 1579, William I.; 1596, Maximilian the Great; 1651, Ferdinand and Mary 1679, Maximilian-Emanuel; 1726, Charles Albert; 1745, Maximilian Joseph I; 1778, Charles, Theodore; 1799, Maximilian-Joseph II, made King Oct. 1805, as Maximilian Joseph I; 1825, Louis, Abd. Mar. 21, '48; 1848 Maximilian Joseph II; 1864, Louis I. (son), heir his brother, Otho, born April 27, 1848.

ARITHMETIC is said to have been introduced from Egypt into Greece by Thales, 600 B.C. The first treatise on, by Euclid. 300 B.C. The "figures" were known to the Arabian Moors about A.D. 900; into Spain, 1050; and into England, 1253 (?)

PAPER is said to have been invented in China, 170 A.D. First made of cotton about 600 & of rags about A.D. 1300 BANK, from "Banco", a bench put in the "market-place" for the exchange of money. The first Bank established was in Italy, in 1808, by the Lombard Jews who soon settled in Lombard Street, London.

BURNING ALIVE WITCHES

HAROUN-AL-RASCHID, 25th CALIPH.

KAABA and TEMPLE. Claimed to have been built by Abraham at Mecca (40 miles from the Red Sea. Quarter of a mile around.)

BEDE. 63, "The Venerable." Born in Northumbria, England. A great Writer and Scholar.

OXFORD UNIVERSITY founded by Alfred the Great. CAMBRIDGE UNIVERSITY by Siegbert about 630, restored by 915

COSMAS. Egyptian Monk of the beginning of the sixth century, wrote a work on the "Topography of the World" to refute the "impious doctrine of the earth's sphericity." He argued that the earth was a vast plain, surrounded by an immense wall at whose side there was a great mountain which concealed the sun every night.

ANCIENT SAVAGE BRITONS.

RESTORED STONEHENGE, WILTSHIRE (ENGLAND). An ancient Temple of the Britons, in which the Druids officiated.

CELTIC HOUSES OF FRANCE, 500 B.C. to A.D. 600

CHARIOT OF THE "LAZY KINGS" OF FRANCE. Sixth and seventh centuries.

"FATHERS." From the "Latin & Greek Fathers" we obtain extracts and a synopsis of many of the more ancient writers, whose works are now lost. They thus become a connecting link to us in the historic chain.

ST. AUGUSTINE Arrives in England 596, 40 monks, sent by Gregory the Great.

MOSQUE BUILT BY OMAR, 637. On the site of Solomon's Temple. Jerusalem was taken by Titus A.D. 70, and razed to the ground, and more than 1,000,000 Jews perished. It was taken by the Saracens, 637, and by the Crusaders in 1099, and 70,000 "Infidels" slain. It was taken by Saladin, of Egypt 1187, and by the Turks in 1516.

(FROM A PHOTOGRAPH)

CAMBRIDGE UNIVERSITY. FOUNDED 630?

BATTLE OF TOURS, OCTOBER 10, 732. Charles Martel defeated the Saracens and saved Europe from Asiatic civilization

FEUDAL SYSTEM Existed from the Seventh

ST. PATRICK IN IRELAND, about A.D. 432.

Vth ECUMENICAL COUNCIL At Constantinople 553

Timeline markers

| 5 | 6 | 7 | 8 |

IVth BC. COUNCIL At CHALCEDON. 451. 50

Vth BC. COUNCIL At Constantinople, Nov. 7, 680 to Feb. 28, 681, vs. Monothelites.

The Romans leave Britain about A.D. 426, when the Picts and Scots invade from the north. The Saxons being invited over to assist in expelling them, gradually take possession of the country, and the Saxon Heptarchy is formed, and exists till Egbert forms the Kingdom of England in 827.

THE COUNTRY CALLED BRITAIN. THE PEOPLE BRITONS.

BRITANNIA

KINGS OF WALES

IRELAND. ST. PATRICK arrived about 432 A.D.

BRITAIN. SAXON HEPTARCHY.

SOME 300 YEARS Called ENGLAND

IRELAND.

NORTHUMBRIA

WESSEX, (WEST SAXONS)

SUSSEX. SOUTH SAXON

KENT

ATTILA and the HUNS.

ATTILA Attila invaded, near 300,000 foot. His was the last great battle fought by the Romans. Rome captured by Alaric, 410, & subjected to six days pillage. He dies 410.

ATTILA dies, 453. "THE SCOURGE OF GOD."

SCANDINAVIA.

BELISARIUS begging his daily Bread.

BELISARIUS. Justinian's great General. He was the hero of many successful campaigns & battles with Italy, Persia, &c. Dies 565, aged 84 years.

The "HEGIRA", Mecca to Medina, Thursday night, July 15, 622.

"Era of the Hegira" begins July 16, 622

The "HEGIRA." 622.

VISIGOTHIC SPAIN.

OSTROGOTHIC MONARCHY OF ITALY CAPITALS, RAVENNA & VERONA.

LOMBARDS, from the North, LOMBARD Kingdom of ITALY

ROMAN or WESTERN EMPIRE CAPITALS, MILAN & RAVENNA.

EASTERN EMPIRE.

GREEK or EASTERN EMPIRE.

THEODOSIUS II.

JUSTINIAN, 38. Marries Theodora, an actress and courtesan. "Justinian code" formed by 10 Artys under Tribonian, 554.

HERACLIUS, 31

CONSTANTINE IV.

SARACEN

MAHOMET commenced preaching, 610. HEGIRA, 622, Mecca to Medina. 531. Justinian pays Persia an annual tribute of 440,000 pieces of gold for "The Nativity of Christ"

KORAN 610

MAHOMET HEGIRA 622.

CHINA.

| AD 500 | AD 600 | AD 700 | AD 800 |

Tribes and civilizations

The Great Wall of China

The first emperor Ch'in Shih Huang Ti united China in 221 BC and established the Ch'in Dynasty from which China takes its name.

The construction of the Great Wall began in 214 BC.

The wall extends about 1,500 miles from the Gulf of Chihli on the Yellow Sea to the gates of central Asia.

It was built of earth and stone with its eastern sections faced with brick.

In later modifications the wall was made some 9 metres (30 feet) high and wide enough for troops to march along, with 12 metre (40 foot) towers at regular intervals. In fact, this newer wall encompassed less territory than the original Great Wall.

The Great Wall of China was built to keep out the Tartars who invaded from the north. The longest wall in the world, it is the most massive construction task ever undertaken by the human race and the only one recognizable from outer space!

People in the New World

At about 20,000 BC, reduced sea levels meant that the Bering Straits became dry land and people crossed into the New World from Siberia. As farming developed, especially with the improved cultivation of maize, so different communities and cultures became established.

New World cultures

Olmec sculpture

1000-600 BC
Olmecs: Mexican Gulf Coast plain
Zapoteks in Monte Alban area

300 BC-AD 550
Hopewell chiefdoms in Ohio and Illinois, North America

Mayan temple

AD 250
Classic Mayan civilization begins

AD 400-900
Teutihuacán have direct control of central Mexico and over part of Guatemala

European tribes

Celts were ancient barbarian tribes widespread in transalpine Europe and the Iberian peninsula. In the 4th and 3rd century BC they expanded into Italy and the Balkans but by 100 BC were seeking refuge from both the Teutonic onslaught westward over the Rhine and further Roman annexation. They moved west and became isolated into corners of western Europe, principally as Gauls and Bretons in France, and Cornish, Welsh, Irish and Manx in Great Britain.

The Angles were a Germanic tribe that invaded Britain in about AD 450.

The Saxons, according to Ptolemy in AD 150, originated from Schleswig and the Baltic coast and occupied islands near the mouth of the Elbe. Vigorous pirates, they settled on the French coast and expanded overland as far as the Rhine. The Old Saxons remained in Germanic areas but the Angles, Saxons and Jutes had begun the conquest of Britain by AD 449.

The Huns were a nomadic tribe of fierce warriors who invaded the south east of Europe around AD 370 and went on to create a huge empire in central Europe.

Goths apparently originated from Scandinavia but, having conquered the **Vandals** and other Germanic peoples, from about 200-150 BC they migrated from the Vistula River area south of the Baltic Sea to reach the northern and western coasts of the Black Sea by AD 376. **Ostrogoths and Visigoths** went on to create vast kingdoms and migrated into such distant regions as the Ukraine, France, Italy and Spain.

Great achievements

Alexander the Great

Perhaps the most famous ruler and soldier of ancient times and certainly one of the greatest generals ever, Alexander the Great was born in 356 BC.

The son of Philip II of Macedonia and educated by Aristotle, he led his armies to conquer the civilized world as he knew it, overthrowing the Persian Empire, extending his conquests into Egypt and India and establishing Greek Hellenistic culture from Gibraltar to the Punjab.

He was a powerful and ruthless commander but a very clever and imaginative one too who used whatever resources he could in the best way possible whether marching armies, cavalry, navy, javelins, Indian hill tribes or elephants. A great statesman, organizer and intellectual, he took poets and artists with him and would exhibit Greek athletics and art to those he subjugated.

Alexander died in Babylon, leaving no heir, at the age of thirty-two. His body was sealed in a glass coffin, encased in gold and preserved in Alexandria, Egypt (the city that was founded and named after him) but this tomb has yet to be discovered.

Although his great Empire rapidly disintegrated after his death, Alexander III's conquests had opened up to the Greeks (and later to the Romans) all the resources of the Middle East, taking Greek culture beyond the Mediterranean. He was worshipped as a god, established over seventy new cities and was the first man to have his portrait on Greek coins. Poised to invade Arabia, his twelve-year reign ended abruptly when he was taken ill after a great banquet and drinking session.

His sudden death may have been due to malaria. Alexander the Great had never lost a battle.

The lighthouse (or Pharos) at Alexandria was one of the seven wonders of the world. The city was named after Alexander the Great

The spread of Christianity

At a time when much of the western world was dominated by the Roman Empire, the new Christian faith took root initially in Palestine where Jesus of Nazareth, at the age of thirty, began his mission, preaching that the kingdom of God was at hand. He travelled mainly through Galilee before His trial and crucifixion in Jerusalem.

Following Christ's death and Resurrection, the disciples continued this ministry but it was Saint Paul, after his conversion on the road to Damascus in AD 38, who undertook the most ambitious voyages and travels, carrying the Christian faith throughout the Mediterranean and covering over 20,000 miles in four separate journeys. When Emperor Constantine 1, the Great, adopted the Christian faith in AD 313 it became part of the Roman establishment.

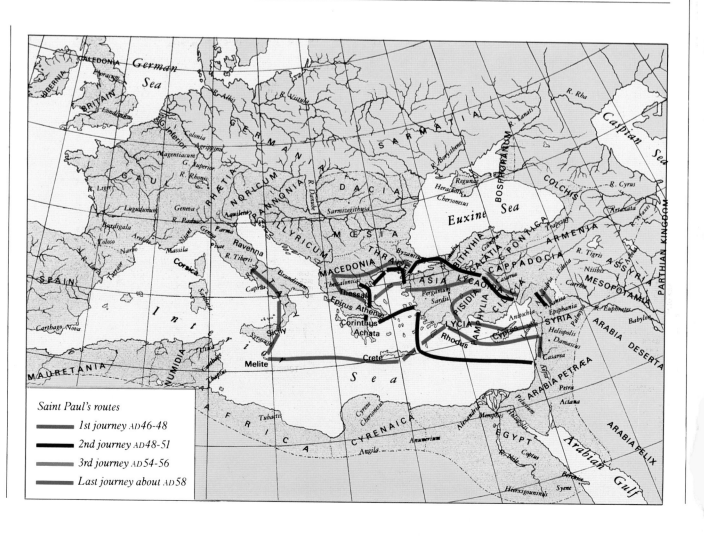

Saint Paul's routes
- *1st journey* AD 46-48
- *2nd journey* AD 48-51
- *3rd journey* AD 54-56
- *Last journey about* AD 58

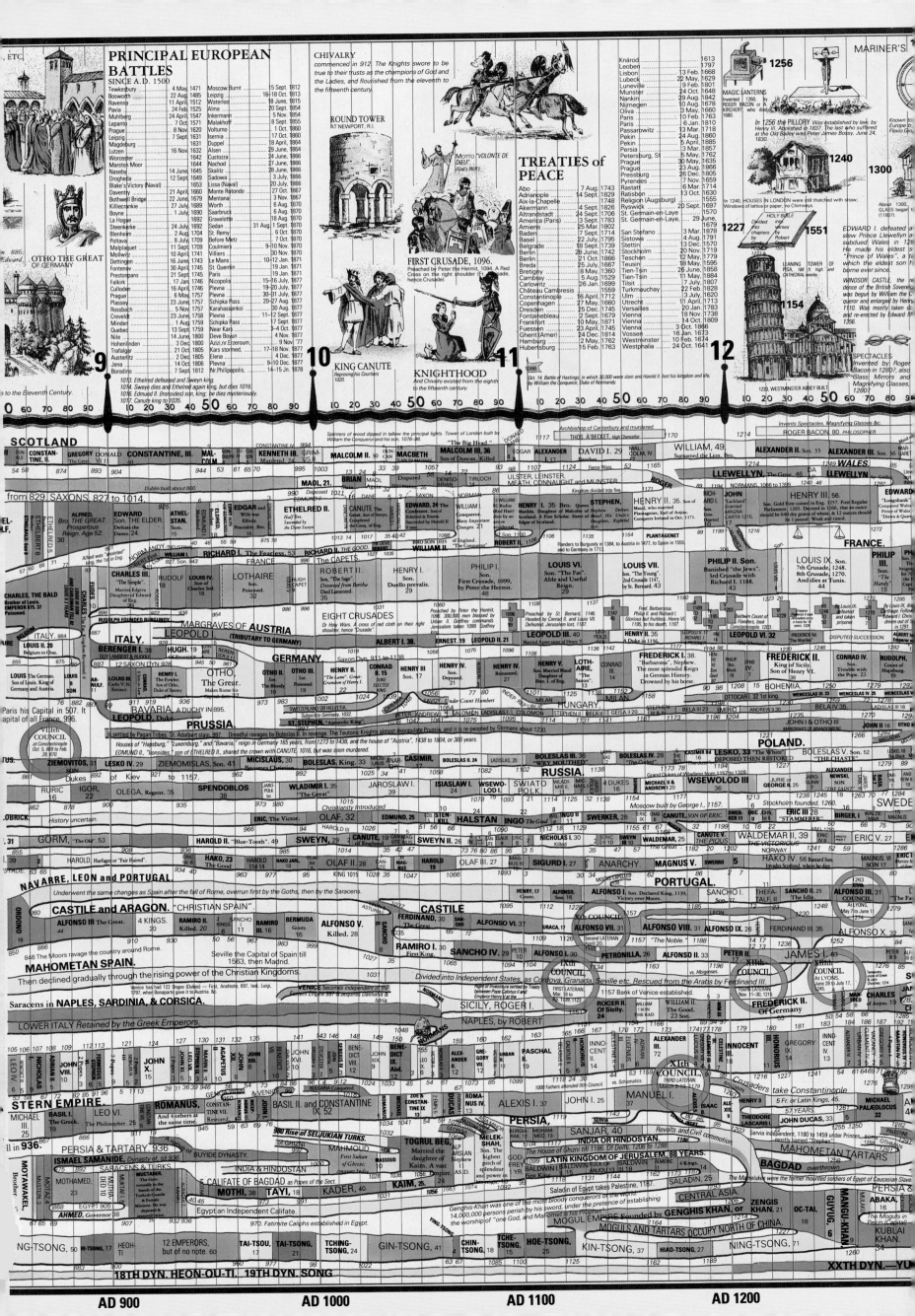

PRINCIPAL EUROPEAN BATTLES
SINCE A.D. 1500

Tewkesbury	4 May, 1471	Moscow Burnt	15 Sept. 1812
Boswroth	22 Aug, 1485	Leipzig	16-18 Oct. 1813
Ravenna	11 April, 1512	Waterloo	18 June, 1815
Pavia	24 Feb. 1525	Alma	20 Sept. 1854
Muhlberg	24 April, 1547	Inkerman	5 Nov. 1854
Lepanto	7 Oct. 1571	Volturno	1 Oct. 1860
Prague	8 Nov. 1620	Malakhoff	8 Sept. 1860
Leipzig	7 Sept. 1631	Isernia	18 April, 1861
Magdeburg	10 May, 1631	Duppel	18 April, 1864
Lutzen	16 Nov. 1632	Alsen	29 June, 1864
Worcester	1642	Custozza	24 June, 1866
Marston Moor	1644	Nachod	27 June, 1866
Naseby	14 June, 1645	Skalitz	28 June, 1866
Drogheda	1649	Sadowa	3 July, 1866
Blake's Victory (Naval)	1653	Lissa (Naval)	20 July, 1866
Dunbar	21 April, 1650	Monte Rotondo	27 Oct. 1867
Bothwell Bridge	22 June, 1679	Mentana	3 Nov. 1867
Killiecrankie	27 July, 1689	Worth	6 Aug. 1870
Boyne	1 July, 1690	Saarbruck	2 Aug. 1870
La Hogue	1692	Gravelotte	18 Aug. 1870
Steenkerke	24 July, 1692	Sedan	31 Aug. 1 Sept. 1870
Blenheim	2 Aug. 1704	St. Remy	1 Oct. 1870
Malplaquet	8 July, 1709	Before Metz	7 Oct. 1870
Mollwitz	10 April, 1741	Coulmiers	9-10 Nov. 1870
Dettingen	30 April, 1745	Villiers	30 Nov. 1870
Fontenoy	30 April, 1745	Le Mans	10-12 Jan. 1871
Prestonpans	21 Sept. 1745	St. Quentin	19 Jan. 1871
Falkirk	16 April, 1746	Nicopolis	15-16 July, 1877
Culloden	6 May, 1757	Plevna	19-20 July, 1877
Prague	6 May, 1757	Plevna	30-31 July, 1877
Plassey	23 June, 1757	Schipka Pass	20-27 Aug. 1877
Rossbach	5 Nov. 1757	Karahassankoi	31 Aug. 1877
Creveldt	23 June, 1758	Plevna	11-12 Sept. 1877
Minden	1 Aug. 1759	Schipka Pass	17-19 Sept. 1877
Quebec	13 Sept. 1759	Gorny Dubnik	24 Oct. 1877
Nile	1 Aug. 1798	Deve Boyun	4 Nov. 1877
Hohenlinden	3 Dec. 1800	Azizi.nr.Erzeroum	9 Nov. 1877
Trafalgar	21 Oct. 1805	Kars stormed,	17-18 Nov. 1877
Austerlitz	2 Dec. 1805	Plevna	10 Dec. 1877
Jena	14 Oct. 1806	Plevna	9-10 Dec. 1877
Borodino	7 Sept. 1812	Nr.Philippolis,	14-15 Jan. 1878

CHIVALRY
commenced in 912 The Knights swore to be true to their trusts as the champions of God and the Ladies, and flourished from the eleventh to the fifteenth century.

ROUND TOWER AT NEWPORT, R.I.

Motto VOLONTE DE DIEU, (God's Will.)

FIRST CRUSADE, 1096.
Preached by Peter the Hermit, 1094. A Red Cross on the right shoulder (Fr. Crusade, hence Crusade)

KING CANUTE
Reproving his Courtiers 1020.

KNIGHTHOOD
And Chivalry existed from the eighth to the fifteenth century.

TREATIES of PEACE

Abo	7 Aug. 1743	Knärod	1613
Adrianople	14 Sept. 1829	Lisbon	1797
Aix-la-Chapelle	1748	Lubeck	22 May, 1629
Akermann	4 Sept. 1826	Luneville	9 Feb. 1801
Altranstadt	24 Sept. 1706	Munster	24 Oct. 1648
America (Paris)	3 Sept. 1783	Nankin	29 Aug. 1842
Amiens	25 Mar. 1802	Nimeguen	10 Aug. 1678
Baden	7 Sept. 1714	Oliva	3 May, 1660
Basel	5 April, 1795	Paris	10 Feb. 1763
Belgrade	18 Sept. 1739	Paris	6 Jan. 1810
Berlin	28 June, 1878	Passarowitz	1 Mar. 1718
Berlin	21 Oct. 1866	Pekin	24 Aug. 1860
Breda	1667	Pekin	5 April, 1885
Bretigny	8 May, 1360	Persia	3 Mar. 1857
Cambray	5 Aug. 1529	Petersburg, St	9 May, 1635
Carlowitz	26 Jan. 1699	Prague	30 May, 1635
Château Cambresis	1559	Prague	23 Aug. 1866
Constantinople	8 April, 1712	Pressburg	26 Dec. 1805
Copenhagen	27 May, 1660	Pyrenees	7 Nov. 1659
Dresden	25 Dec. 1745	Rastatt	6 Mar. 1714
Fontainebleau	2 Sept. 1679	Ratisbon	13 Oct. 1630
Frankfort	10 May, 1871	Religion (Augsburg)	1555
Fuessen	23 April, 1745	Ryswick	20 Sept. 1697
Ghent (Amer)	24 Dec. 1814	St. Germain-en-Laye	1679
Hamburg	2 May, 1762	St. Germain-en-Laye	29 June,
Hubertsburg	15 Feb. 1763	San Stefano	3 Mar. 1878
		Sistowa	4 Aug. 1791
		Stockholm	13 Dec. 1570
		Stockholm	21 Nov. 1719
		Teschen	12 May, 1779
		Tien-Tsin	18 May, 1565
		Tien-Tsin	26 June, 1858
		Tien-Tsin	11 May, 1884
		Tilsit	7 July, 1807
		Turun-auchay	22 Feb. 1828
		Utrecht	11 April, 1713
		Versailles	20 Jan. 1783
		Vienna	3 Oct. 1735
		Vienna	14 Oct. 1809
		Vienna	1 July, 1620
		Vienna	3 Oct. 1866
		Vossem	16 Jan. 1673
		Westminster	10 Feb. 1674
		Westphalia	24 Oct. 1641

MARINER'S

1256 In 1256 the PILLORY Was established by Henry II. Abolished in 1837. The last who suffered at the Old Bailey was Peter James Bossy, June 24, 1830.

MAGIC LANTERNS Invented 1260, by ROGER BACON, or KIRCHER? 1680.

1240 In 1240, HOUSES in LONDON were still thatched with straw; Windows of lattice or paper, no Chimneys.

1300 About 1300, GLASS began to be used (1180?)

HOLY BIBLE Divided into chapters by Robert

1227

1551

1154 LEANING TOWER OF PISA, 188 ft. high and CATHEDRAL.

EDWARD I. defeated a slew Prince Llewellyn an subdued Wales in 12. He made his eldest S "Prince of Wales," a which the eldest son borne ever since.

WINDSOR CASTLE, the dence of the British Sovere was begun by William the queror and enlarged by Henr 1110. Was mostly rebuilt a and re-erected by Edward I 1356.

SPECTACLES Invented by Roger Bacon in 1280?, also Glass, Mirrors and Magnifying Glasses, 1280?

1220, WESTMINSTER ABBEY BUILT

Timeline reference marks: 9, 10, 11, 12

Inventing Spectacles, Magnifying Glasses &c. ROGER BACON, 80, PHILOSOPHER

SCOTLAND
CONSTANTINE III. MALCOLM KENNETH III. GRIM-US 8 MALCOLM II. 30 MACBETH MALCOLM III. 36 Son of Duncan, Killed. Edgar Alexander DAVID I. 29 Brother WILLIAM, 49. Surnamed the Lion. Bro. ALEXANDER II. Son. 35 ALEXANDER III. Son. 36 MAR-GARET

GREGORY DONALD CONSTANTINE III. Son of Ethelred and Sweyn king.

WALES

LLEWELLYN The Great, 46 DA LLEWELLYN

from 829. SAXONS 827 to 1014.

ALFRED, THE GREAT. Prosperous Reign. Age 52. EDWARD THE ELDER. Son. 24. ATHEL-STAN. Son. EDMUND I. ELDRED Bro. EDWY Son EDGAR and Bro. Peaceable. Bro. ETHELRED II. Half Bro. CANUTE The Great, Son of Ethelred & Emma. Succeeded by Harold II EDWARD, 24 The Confessor. Son of Ethelred & Emma. Succeeded by Harold II. WILLIAM I William (Red Hair) of Scotland. HENRY I. 35 Son of Malcolm of Scotland. A Fine Scholar. Sister of Malcolm III. Daughter, Rightful STEPHEN. Nephew. Defrays Plantagenet, Earl of Anjou. Conquers Ireland in Oct. 1171. RICH-ARD I. JOHN "Lackland" Granted MAGNA CARTA 1215. HENRY III. 56. Son of John. First Regular Parliament, 1265. Decreed in 1266, that an ounce should be 640 dry grains of wheat. 12 ounces should = 1 pound; Weak and timid. EDWARD

NORMANDY. FRANCE.

RICHARD I. The Fearless, 53 RICHARD II. The GOOD. ROBERT II. WILLIAM I. "The Conqueror." WILLIAM II. PLANTAGENET Flanders to Burgundy in 1384, to Austria in 1477, to Spain in 1555 and to Germany in 1713.

FRANCE.
CHARLES III. "The Simple." Married Edgiva Daughter of Edward of King. RUDOLF LOUIS IV. Son of Charles 3rd. 18 LOTHAIRE HUGH CAPET ROBERT II. "The Sage". Divorced from Bertha Died Lamented. HENRY I. Son. PHILIP I. Son. First Crusade, 1099, by Peter the Hermit. LOUIS VI. Son. "The Fat" Able and Useful Reign. LOUIS VII. Son. "The Young". 2nd Crusade 1147, by St. Bernard. 43 PHILIP II. Son. Banished "the Jews" 3rd Crusade with Richard I. 1188. 43 LOUIS IX. Son. 7th Crusade, 1248. 8th Crusade, 1270. And dies at Tunis. 44 PHILIP III.

CHARLES THE BALD. King of Italy. EMPEROR 875. 37 Poisoned. THE CAPETS.

ITALY.
LOUIS II. 20 BERENGER I. 20 HUGH. ITALY. 884 ITALY. RUDOLPH FOUNDED BURGUNDY MARGRAVES OF AUSTRIA LEOPOLD (TRIBUTARY TO GERMANY) ALBERT I. 38. ERNEST. 19 LEOPOLD II. 21 LEOPOLD III. HENRY V. A Duke in 1156. LEOPOLD VI. 32 FREDERICK IId. "The Warlike"

EIGHT CRUSADES Or Holy Wars. A cross of red cloth on their right shoulder, hence "Crusade." Preached by Peter the Hermit, 1060, when blessed by Urban II. Godfrey commands. Jerusalem taken 1099. Godfrey Preached by St. Bernard, 1108, Headed by Conrad II, and Louis VII. Jerusalem, lost, 1187. Fred. Barbarossa, Philip II. and Richard I. Glorious but fruitless. Henry VI. 1195, by his death, 1197. Baldwin Count of Flanders, took Constantinople. 1203

GERMANY.
Saxon Dyn. 911 to 1138 OTHO The Great. Makes Rome his HENRY I. The Fowler. Son of Otho. Duke of Saxony OTHO II. The Bloody. OTHO III. HENRY II. "The Lame", Great-Grandson of Henry I. CONRAD II. Son. HENRY III. Son. HENRY IV. Deposed. 21 HENRY IV. Reinstated. LOTH-AIRE "The Saxon". CONRAD III FREDERICK I. 38. "Barbarossa". The most splendid Reign in German History. Drowned by his horse. HENRY VI. A Duke in 1156. FREDERICK II. King of Sicily, Son of Henry VI. CONRAD IV. Son. Trouble with the Pope. 23 RUDOLPH. Count of Hapsburg.

LOUIS The German. Son of Louis. King of Bavaria. ARNULF. CARLO V.N Extinct. CONRAD Son of Otho, Duke of Saxony

BAVARIA, A DUCHY in 895. SWITZERLAND OR HELVETIA Subject to Germany, 1032 HUNGARY. ST. STEPHEN "The Apostolic King" MILAN BOHEMIA OTTOCAR. 32 1st king. WENCESLAS. 23 WENCESLAS III 25 WENCESLAS

Paris his Capital in 507. It apital of all France, 996. LEOPOLD Duke PRUSSIA It settled by Pagan Saxons. St. Adalbert slain, 897. Dreadful ravages by Boleslas II. in revenge. The Teutonic Knights almost depopulate Prussia, and it is re-peopled by Germans about 1230.

POLAND.
ZIEMOVITUS, 31 LESKO IV. 29 ZIEMOMISLAS, Son. 41 MICISLAUS, 30 BOLESLAS, King. 33 CASIMIR BOLESLAS II. 24 BOLESLAS III. 36 "Wry Mouthed" BOLESLAS IV. 28 "The Curled" CASIMIR IId LESKO, 33 "The White" DEPOSED THEN RESTORED BOLESLAS V. Son. 52 "The Chaste" LESKO

EDMUND II. "Ironsides", Brother of ETHELRED II., shared the crown with CANUTE 1016, but was soon murdered.

RUSSIA.
Dukes of Kiev 921 to 1157. RURIC IGOR OLEGA, Regent. SPENDOBLOS WLADIMIR I. 35 "The Great" JAROSLAW I. 39 ISIASLAW I. WSEWO-LOD I. SWIATO POLK WLADI-MIR II. MICHAEL II & ANDREW I JURIE or GEORGE II. 25 ALEXANDER NEWSKI, SON OF JAROSLAW WSEWOLOD III

Christianity Introduced Mahometan. Moscow built by George I., 1157. Stockholm founded, 1255.

SWEDE
ERIC, The Victor. OLAF, 32 EDMUND, 25 STEN-KILL HALSTAN INGO The Good INGO II SWERKER CANUTE Son of ERIC. ERIC III 28 "STAMMERER" BIRGER I.

GORM, "The Old". 53 HAROLD II. "Blue-Tooth". 49 SWEYN, 29 CANUTE of England SWEYN II. 26 NICHOLAS I. 30 ERIC SWEYN WALDEMAR, 25 CANUTE The Great WALDEMAR II, 39 THE VICTORIOUS ERIC V. 27

HAROLD Harfager or "Fair Haired". HAKO I. The Good HAROLD HAKO JARL OLAF I. 28 OLAF II. 28 HAROLD SIGURD I. 27 ANARCHY. MAGNUS V. SWERRO HAKO IV. 56 Bastard Son. Invades Scotland MAGNUS VI. SON 17

NAVARRE, LEON and PORTUGAL.
Underwent the same changes as Spain after the fall of Rome, overrun first by the Goths, then by the Saracens.

PORTUGAL. HENRY, 17 Count. ALFONSO, 30 Son. ALFONSO I. Son. Declared King, 1139, Victory over Moors. SANCHO I. SANCHO II. "The Idle" ALFONSO III. 31 COUNCIL

CASTILE and ARAGON. "CHRISTIAN SPAIN".
ALFONSO III The Great. 44 4 KINGS. RAMIRO II. Killed. 20 BERMUDA III. ALFONSO V. Killed. 20 SANCHO CASTILE FERDINAND, 30 The Great URACA, 17 ALFONSO VI. 37 ALFONSO VII. 31 ALFONSO VIII. 31 ALFONSO IX. 31 ALFONSO X. 26 FERDINAND III. 30 ALFONSO X. 32

RAMIRO I. First King. SANCHO IV. ALFONSO I. 30 PETRONILLA, 26 ALFONSO II. 33 PETER II. JAMES I. Second LATERAN April 20 "The Noble." 1188 XIth COUNCIL XIIth COUNCIL AT LYONS, June 28 to July 17, 1245.

MAHOMETAN SPAIN.
Then declined gradually through the rising power of the Christian Kingdoms. Seville the Capital of Spain till 1563, then Madrid. Divided into Independent States, as Cordova, Granada, Seville etc. Rescued from the Arabs by Ferdinand IV IXth COUNCIL

Venice had had 122 Doges (Dukes) — First, Anafeste, 697, Last, Luigi, 1797, when Bonaparte gave it to Austria. &c. VENICE becomes independent of the Eastern Empire 697. & Jacques Dalmatia & Istria. 1157 Bank of Venice established.

Saracens in NAPLES, SARDINIA, & CORSICA. SICILY, ROGER I. ROGER II Of Sicily. 24 WILLIAM I Son 20 WILLIAM II. The Good. 23 Son. FREDERICK II. Of Germany CHARLES Of Anjou. 28.

LOWER ITALY Retained by the Greek Emperors. NAPLES, by Robert. NORMANS

STERN EMPIRE.
MICHAEL III. 25 BASIL II. The Greek. LEO VI. The Philosopher. 25 ROMANUS, And 4 others at the same time. CONSTANTINE VII. Restored. BASIL II. and CONSTANTINE IX. 52 ZOE & CONSTANTINE CONSTANTINE IX DUCAS ROMANUS IV. ALEXIS I. 37 JOHN I. 25 MANUEL I. Crusaders take Constantinople ISAAC HENRY Theodore Lascaris THEODORE LASCARIS JOHN DUCAS, 33 MICHAEL PALÆOLOCUS 22

PERSIA & TARTARY. 936. PERSIA, 980 Rise of SELJUKIAN TURKS. SANJAR, 40 Revolts and Civil commotion. MAHOMETAN TARTARS

ISMAEL SAMANIDE, Dynasty of, till 936. SARACENS & TURKS. MAHMOUD OF GHIZNI TOGRUL BEG. Married the daughter of Kaim. A vast MELEK-SHAH. Son. The highest pitch of splendour and power in A.S.D. The House of Ghizni 1186. Of Delhi, 1206 to 1288 INDIA OR HINDOSTAN. LATIN KINGDOM OF JERUSALEM, 88 YEARS. BAGDAD overthrown

CALIFATE OF BAGDAD as Popes of the Sect. MOTHI, 38 TAYI, 18 KADER, 40 KAIM, 25 INDIA & HINDOSTAN Saladin of Egypt takes Palestine, 1197. CENTRAL ASIA. ZENGIS KHAN. 21 OC-TAI.

Egyptian Independent Califate. 970. Fatimite Caliphs established in Egypt. Genghis-Khan was one of the most bloody conquerors of the time, on the pretence of establishing the worship of "one God, and Mahomet is his Prophet" MOGUL EMPIRE Founded by GENGHIS KHAN, or MANGU-KHAN. The Moguls in Pekin 1279. GUYUG, 6 KUBLAI KHAN.

18TH DYN. HEON-OU-TI. 19TH DYN. SONG NG-TSONG, 50 HI-TSONG, 17 HEOH. 12 EMPERORS, but of no note. 60 TAI-TSOU. TAI-TSONG, 24 TCHING-TSONG, 24 GIN-TSONG, 41 CHIN-TSONG, 18 TCHE-TSONG, 15 HOE-TSONG, KIN-TSONG, 37 HIAO-TSONG, 27 NING-TSONG, 71 XXTH DYN.—YU

AD 900   **AD 1000**   **AD 1100**   **AD 1200**

The Vikings

Initially farming communities, from the 8th to the 11th centuries, the Scandinavian peoples became very active traders, dealing in ivory from walrus tusks, furs, skins and slaves, as well as articles made from silver, wood, amber and soapstone. With a growing demand for such goods, the Vikings found it profitable to leave their northern homes to trade and to augment their gains through raid, plunder and piracy. They began to seize new territory in coastal and riverside regions of north and western Europe.

Travelling in fast, manoeuverable longboats, the fierce determination of the warriors and a constant supply of manpower soon gave the Vikings supremacy of the seas.

They founded communities as far afield as Ireland and Russia

They settled as farmers in Greenland, Iceland and Newfoundland

They abounded in islands of the western seas, including the Hebrides, Shetland and Orkney Islands

They established a royal line in Dublin, Ireland and in the Isle of Man

They held a good deal of English land, especially in East Anglia, Mercia and Northumbria

Alfred the Great of Wessex was finally victorious over them in 878

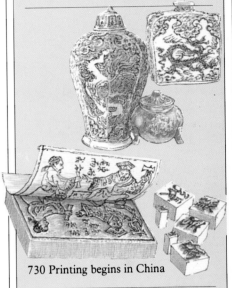

Charlemagne (Charles the Great) (742-814)

King of the Franks from 768 to 814 and Emperor from 800

He inherited a vast sweep of lands curving round in an arc from south-west France to the Netherlands and Germany

Conquered most of the Christian territory in western Europe to create what was to become the Holy Roman Empire

Conquered and converted the Saxons

Took over the Lombard kingdom in northern Italy in 774

Encouraged intellectual pursuits and began the Carolingian Renaissance

Established seats of learning including a school of calligraphy from which a new script, the Carolingian miniscule, was developed and eventually spread right across the Empire

Alfred the Great (849-899)

Became king of Wessex in 871

Defeated the Danes and divided England with them

Reintroduced literature, encouraged learning and scholarship, translated works from Latin into English

Compiled the Anglo Saxon Chronicle, an historical record

Created a code of laws

Organized a system of defence: created a fast mobile army; founded the Navy; built fortified boroughs

Otto I, The Great (912-973)

King of east Francia and Emperor of Germany

Subjugated rebellious brothers 938-9

Marched into Italy 951

Defeated the Magyars in 955

Subdued the Slavs in 960

Crowned Emperor by the Pope in 962

Consolidated his kingdom to provide stability and prosperity

William the Conqueror (c. 1027-1087)

Duke of Normandy and King of England

William, like all Normans, was of Viking descent, the first duke, Rollo, in 911 being officially granted land he had already seized near the Seine

A young and vigorous knight, William spent his early dukedom dispelling anarchy and rebellion to establish a firm hold in Normandy

He defeated King Harold at the Battle of Hastings in 1066 to become king of England

Instigated the first national survey, the *Domesday Book*, 1086

Established a strong feudal hold over England

Genghis Khan (1162-1227)

The son of a tribal chief, he spent his youth in secrecy and poverty, hiding from enemy warriors

He became a great Mongol conqueror

His empire extended from the Pacific to the River Dniepr and the northern shores of the Black Sea

Originally called Temujin, the title he took, Genghis Khan, means Ruler of All Men

He broke through the Great Wall of China to invade the Chin Empire, leading to its eventual destruction

Emperor Kublai Khan who founded the Yüan dynasty in China was his grandson

Religions, conquests and kings

Persecution

During the 13th century Jews were treated very harshly and there were numerous pogroms, or massacres. Of those who survived, many were forced out of Western European countries and settled in Poland and Hungary.

Christian missionaries

432 St Patrick Ireland
550 St David Wales
563 St Columba Iona, Scotland
590 St Columban France
596 St Augustine England
619 St Columban & St Gall Italy
719 St Boniface Germany

Islam

The way in which Islam spread was one of the most important and influential factors in world history.

Born in AD570 in Mecca, Mohammed received his first revelations when he was forty. When his teaching aroused opposition amongst the aristocracy, he gathered his followers together and travelled 280 miles north-east to Medina. Having established and organized his base there he eventually returned to Mecca to cast out idols, to teach others to submit to the will of Allah and, through the Koran, to deliver the word of God.

Mohammed was a prophet, a man who made no claim to be divine, but the religion he initiated spread throughout Arabia and the Hejaz and thence to

Dome of the Rock, Jerusalem, the first great Islamic building, completed in AD692

Persia, Armenia and Oman, into Libya, and northern Africa, to Sumatra and Java, and into Spain and India.

Initially, under the dictates of the Koran, other religious movements were treated with respect but from the 8th century onwards wholesale conversion was enacted by fanatical Arab armies and Islam has remained an important element in wars and international politics ever since.

Buddhism

Gautama Buddha was an Indian prince and a spiritual teacher who lived from 567 to 487BC. The major Oriental religion he had founded taught salvation through ethics and discipline, through right conduct and understanding. In very simplistic terms it teaches that suffering is universal and springs from desire, so the cure is to negate all selfish cravings and attain Nirvana, a transcendential state free from desires, suffering or sorrow.

Buddhism has developed in different ways through different nations and sects. It remained a flourishing vigorous faith in India until about AD 500 and was established in Japan in AD 594 when the Regent Shōtoku Taishi sought to use its ideals to establish unity between contentious clans. By the 8th century AD it had been absorbed into Tibet and was prevalent over the whole of Burma by the 12th century. Zen Buddhism emerged in China in the 7th century AD, being called Ch'an; the Japanese pronunciation of this is zen.

Hinduism

The major religion in the Indian sub-continent, Hinduism prescribes a way of life and social system based on the caste system. Emerging gradually from

various sacrificial cults of ancient times brought in by Aryan invaders, through hymns and incantations known as Vedas, with sacred writings called the Brahamanas (about 700 BC), Hinduism proper evolved between 600 and 200 BC. The worship of feminine divinities was established by AD 650. The Mother Goddess, Shiva the destroyer and Vishnu the preserver became the three great classical divinities although there are many others, including Brahma the Creator. The philospher Sankara in about AD 800 was a great exponent of the faith. A complex religion developed: Brahma alone is real — the spiritual, the essence of all things and the void which is the source of life and joy; material appearances are an illusion and truth can be discovered only by inner contemplation; many animals, plants and natural objects are considered sacred and there is belief in the trasmigration of souls.

The Crusades

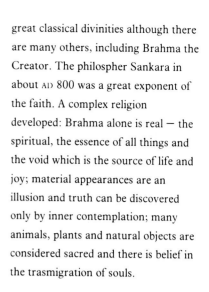

Soldiers, ill-disciplined fighting men, pilgrims, clergymen, entire families, monks, freed criminals, landless knights: all types of men and women flocked in response to Pope Urban II's call to the first crusade. For almost the next two hundred years mass migrations under the crusadal banner swept to the East and back again, to fight the Holy War, hoping to drive back the Turks, to free the sacred places and to gain honour, salvation or riches. A kingdom was established in Jerusalem, a pricipality in Antioch, and countships in Edessa and Tripoli.

1st Crusade began in 1096: took Jerusalem in 1099 Edessa fell in 1144 and this led to . . .

2nd Crusade 1147: laid siege to Damascus in 1148 but this was a fiasco and was abandoned after only four days. Saladin conquered Jerusalem in 1187

3rd Crusade began 1189 led by Richard 1 of England (the Lionheart), Philip II of France and Frederick I (Barbarossa) of Germany and Holy Roman Empire: regained coast south of Acre and secured Cyprus

4th Crusade 1199: Latin emperor set up in Constantinople

5th Crusade 1218: attacked Egypt, taking Damietta in 1219 but ceded this in 1221 after army trapped by Nile flood

6th Crusade 1227: led by Frederick II: gained Jerusalem, Nazareth, Sidon and Lydda Jerusalem recaptured by Turks in 1244

7th Crusade: 1248, led by Louis IX of France; took Damietta, Egypt in 1250 but Louis was captured and ceded Damietta in 1250. From 1250 Mameluke sultans of Egypt dominate the Latin east

8th Crusade 1267 led by Louis IX of France. Diverted to Tunisia, he died there in 1270

Year	Event	Year	Event
1901	Trans-Siberian railway opened.	1967	First successful human heart transplant.
1903	Suffragette Movement founded.		Arab-Israeli 'Six Day War'.
1904-5	Russo-Japanese War.	1968	Civil rights leader Ma[rtin]
1905	Albert Einstein states First Theory of Relativity.		Luther King assassinated.
1906	San Francisco earthquake.		Students riot in Paris. Students in US and
1908	Ford's Model T automobile.		Europe protest about Vietnam War.
	Scout Movement founded.		USSR suppresses 'Prague Spring' in
1909	Louis Blériot flies across English Channel.	1969	Czechoslovakia. Concorde, world's fi[rst]
1910	Marie Curie's treatise on radiography.		supersonic passenge[r] aircraft.
1912	Loss of RMS Titanic.		Apollo 11 (USA) land[s]
1914	Panama Canal opens. First World War begins.		first men on moon.
1915	Gas first used in war.	1970	Boeing 747 (Jumbo) now in service.
1917	Russian Revolution.	1973	US troops withdraw from Vietnam.
1919	The atom is split.		'Yom-Kippur'
1919/20	League of Nations founded.		Arab-Israeli war.
1922	British Broadcasting Corporation founded.	1974	US President Nixon forced to resign over
	Insulin treatment for diabetes developed.		'Watergate' scandal.
	Tutankhamen's tomb discovered.	1976	Milan chemical plant disaster.
1923	Adolf Hitler's Munich putsch fails.	1977	Astronomers observ[e] rings around Uranus.
1926	General Strike in UK.	1978	World's first 'test tub[e]' baby born (UK).
1927	First talking movie. Lindbergh flies from New York to Paris.		Camp David Treaty (Israel and Egypt).
1928	Alexander Fleming discovers penicillin.	1979	Three Mile Island nuclear power plant leaks radiation.
1929	Wall Street stock market crash.		US bid to rescue hostages in Iran fails.
1930	R101 airship disaster Gas turbine invented.		Mount St Helens volcano erupts in US.
1931	Floods in China.	1981	US space shuttle launched.
1932	Sydney Harbour Bridge opened.		Attempted assassination of Pop[e]
1933	Adolf Hitler becomes German Chancellor.		John Paul II. President Sadat of
1935	Radar invented.		Egypt assassinated.
1936-9	Spanish Civil War.		
1939	First jet aircraft. Germany invades Poland: Second World War begins.	1982	Israel invades south Lebanon.
		1983	USSR shoots down Korean Air Lines passenger plane.
1942	First nuclear reactor.		
1943	Colossus 1, the first programmable electronic computer.	1984	IRA attempt to assassinate British cabinet.
	Aqualung invented.		Famine in Ethiopia, Sudan, Chad.
1945	Atomic bomb used.	1986	US space shuttle Challenger disaster.
1946	First meeting of United Nations General Assembly.		Chernobyl nuclear disaster in USSR.
1947	Dead Sea Scrolls discovered.	1987	US and USSR agree eliminate intermedia[te]
	First supersonic air flight.		range nuclear missi[les] Crash in world stock
1948	Mahatma Gandhi assassinated.		markets.
	Transistor invented.	1988	Iran-Iraq War ends.
1948-9	Israeli War of Independence.		Earthquake destroys towns in Armenia.
1949	NATO alliance formed.	1989	Californian earthqua[ke]
1950	Korean War begins.		Violent suppression [of] army of student pro[test]
1952	Hydrogen bomb tested.		in China.
1953	Mount Everest climbed.		Protests and revolu[tion] in Eastern Bloc:
	Netherlands flood disaster.		dismantling of Berlin Wall.
	Structure of DNA discovered.		
1954	First nuclear power station (USSR).	1990	Nelson Mandela released after 25 ye[ars]
	Bannister breaks 4-minute mile barrier.		in jail in South Afric[a]. East and West Germ[any]
1955	Hovercraft invented.		re-unite.
1956	Egypt nationalizes Suez canal: this leads to war.		Iraqi troops invade Kuwait.
	Hungarian uprising suppressed by Soviet troops.		French and British Channel Tunnel bor[ing] holes meet.
1957	Sputnik 1, first orbiting satellite, launched. Treaty of Rome inaugurates EEC.	1991	The Gulf War: US an[d] UK forces liberate Kuwait from Iraq.
1959	St Lawrence seaway opened.		Ravij Gandhi assassinated.
1960	Laser invented.		Gorbachev resigns communist rule end[s]
1961	Yuri Gagarin first man in space.		Soviet Union. Yeltsin elected fir[st]
	Berlin Wall erected.		president of Russia.
1962	US troops move to support South Vietnam.		Civil war in Yugosla[via] Dubrovnik besiege[d].
	Cuban Missile Crisis.	1992	Bill Clinton elected President of USA.
1963	President Kennedy (USA) assassinated.		UK's Prince Charles [and]
	Cultural revolution launched in China.		Princess Diana separate.
1965			

Two world wars

The First World War

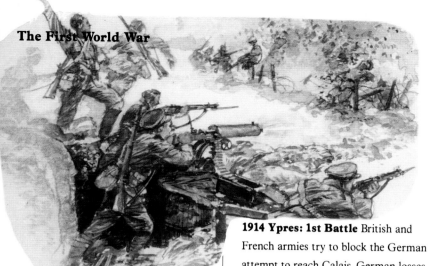

June 1914 Assassination of Archduke Ferdinand at Sarajevo is the spark that turns the lining up of powers into active offensives.

1914 Marne The British and French armies oppose the German invasion of France. Fighting on the western front develops into trench warfare, with opposing armies dug in on a line that stretched for 400 miles, from the Swiss frontier to the English Channel.

1914 war in the air Aeroplanes are initially used for reconnaissance only but before long artillery spotters, bombers and fighters emerge.

1914 Ypres: 1st Battle British and French armies try to block the German attempt to reach Calais. German losses 150,000; British and French losses 100,000.

1915 Ypres: 2nd Battle Poison gas is used for the first time by the Germans.

1916 Verdun Commanded by Crown Prince William, German forces launch a major attack against the French forces. German losses 328,000; French losses 348,000.

1916 Jutland The battle at sea: Despite heavy losses, the British retain command of the North Sea.

1916 The Somme The British and French advance to take 320 square kilometres (125 square miles) of ground. The first tank is used by the British. There are enormous losses

with about 600,000 casualties on both sides. Lives are wasted in vain for the end result is still stalemate.

1917 war at sea German submarine attacks sink one in four ships leaving British ports until the convoy system is set up in May.

1917 Ypres: 3rd Battle 'Passchendaele' Heavy rain turns the battlefields to deep mud. Over four months, the British forces make eight attacks to gain only five miles and lose 400,000 men.

1918 St Mihiel Salient Americans break the German line.

1918 1,480 Allied planes defeat the German air force.

1918 Austria, Turkey and Bulgaria collapse under Allied offensives. The German fleet mutinies and the Kaiser abdicates.

The war ends on 11 November.

The Second World War

1 September 1939 Germany invades Poland

3 September 1939 Britain and France declare they are at war with Germany

June 1940 Dunkirk Evacuation of allied soldiers from Dunkirk

August 1940 Battle of Britain For 114 days the German airforce, with 2,500 plane tries to gain air supremacy over Britain. The RAF, with far fewer planes, resists this attack; for example on 18 August the RAF destroys 694 Luftwaffe planes and loses only 150 of its own.

1941 Pearl Harbor Japanese bomb US Pacific Fleet

1942 Coral Sea and Midway Americans drive back Japanese invasion fleets.

1942 Singapore The great naval base surrenders to the Japanese who

eventually control Burma, the Philippines and Indonesia.

1942 El Alamein British Eighth Army drive German troops from Egypt

1942-1943 Stalingrad 21 German divisions advance 2,300 miles into the Soviet Union and enter Stalingrad. However, by January 1943 they are trapped there and, reduced to 100,000 men from their original 300,000, the

army surrenders.

6 June 1944 'D Day' Allied forces land in Normandy in the biggest ever sea-borne attack.

October 1944 Leyte Gulf US fleet defeats Japanese

1944-1945 Ardennes: the Battle of the Bulge Germans launch their final counter-attack through the Ardennes Forest but suffer enormous losses.

28 April 1945 Mussolini is shot by Italian partisans.

30 April 1945 Adolf Hitler commits suicide in his Berlin bunker.

August 1945 Atom bombs dropped at Hiroshima and Nagasaki in Japan.

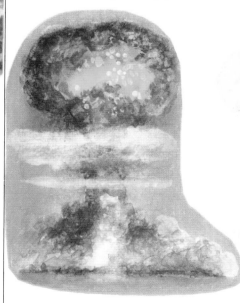

The war is ended. 70 million men fought in the war. Statistics vary but as many as 55 million people may have died, including 8 per cent of the German population, 10 per cent of the Russians, over 13 million Chinese and 6 million Jews (one third of the Jews then living).

Invention and discovery

The Gutenberg press

The Gutenberg press: printing made the Bible widely available for the first time

Since this section of the chart covers six centuries, the changes that took place are far too numerous to discuss in detail but, in particular, the impact of printing in the fourteenth century made the written word more readily available, leading to more opportunity for education and easier distribution of information. This in turn brought religious changes, spearheaded by Luther, and greater political awareness. Overall, the impact of books and newsprint on human society is inestimable.

Martin Luther

From the eighteenth century and into the nineteenth, a spurt of new inventions in the western world led to both the Industrial Revolution with the development of machinery in factories and to new agricultural methods. Both rural and urban lives were changed dramatically, with many people deserting villages to seek work in towns and cities.

By the nineteenth century discoveries and inventions were having an impact in both industrial and domestic life, with the use of electricity and improved communications, while new forms of transportation were taking shape, ready to launch society into the twentieth century.

Meanwhile developments in medicine led to radical changes, both in the understanding of hygiene and the nature of disease and in methods of treatment and prevention.

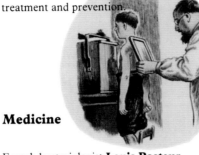

Medicine

French bacteriologist **Louis Pasteur** (1822-95) established the science of bacteriology. He developed methods of pasteurizing milk, preventing anthrax and cholera in animals and innoculating against hydrophobia (rabies) in humans.

Joseph Lister (1827-1912) introduced antiseptics into surgery.

Ignaz Semmelweiss of Vienna and Budapest advised disinfection of hands and clothing which greatly reduced risk of infection and death in hospitals, especially of women after childbirth.

While many had been experimenting with nitrous oxide gas and ether, it was **William Thomas Morton** who satisfactorily demonstrated ether as an effective anaesthetic in Massachusetts in 1846 and **James Young Simpson** of Edinburgh, Scotland who first used chloroform in an operation in 1847.

Wilhelm K Röntgen discovered X-rays in 1895 while Pierre and Marie Curie discovered radium in 1898.

Sigmund Freud (1856-1939) developed the new field of psychiatry.

Struggles for power and independence

Hundred Years War

Intermittent wars between England and France from 1337 until 1453: initially a trade dispute over the wool trade, the antagonism developed into full-scale battles over English claims to the French throne. The Hundred Years War encompassed the Battle of Crécy (1346) won by Edward III and the Battle of Agincourt in 1415 when Henry V defeated the French. In 1429 Joan of Arc rallied the French armies but was captured and burned at the stake in 1431. Ultimately, England's only French possession was Calais.

The Wars of the Roses

From 1455 to 1485 England was the scene of civil war fought between rival branches of the royal line, the house of York (their emblem, a white rose) and the house of Lancaster (the red rose). The wars involved Richard III, Henry VI and Edward IV and ended when the Earl of Richmond (Henry VII) defeated Richard III at Bosworth and subsequently married the daughter of Edward IV, so uniting both houses.

The French Revolution

This began in 1789 with the meeting of the States General at Versailles and was inflamed by waves of simultaneous unrest in different stratas of society: the aristocracy sought a less centralized monarchy, the middle classes a parliamentary type of government and the down-trodden peasants an end to their gross exploitation. During the Terror 300,000 suspects were arrested and 17,000 executed while many more died in prison or were killed without trial.

1789 Storming of Bastille
1792 France is declared a Republic
1793 Louis XVI and Marie Antoinette executed
1793-1794 Reign of Terror
1795 The Directory rules France
1795-96 Rise of Napoleon Bonaparte; a young general, he crushes the Royalists and leads the army to conquer most of Italy

The French Revolution's death toll of executions

Paris: 2,600 (1,515 in June/July 1794)
Angers: 2,000
Nantes: 3,000 + 2,000 drowned
Vendée: Martial law, thousands shot
Lyons: nearly 2,000 executed
Arras, Orange, Marseille and Bordeaux: total 1,300 executions
Toulon: 800 shot

American Civil War (1861-1865)

Begun when the guns of the South opened fire on Federal Fort Sumter and ending with General Robert E. Lee and General Joseph E Johnston's surrender, this war involved some 3,000,000 troops and saw a higher proportion of deaths (21 per cent) than did the First World War. Twice as many soldiers died of disease than in battle. The casualties were 617,000 dead and 375,000 wounded.

The Civil War resulted in the preservation of the Union, changes in the United States constitution and the abolition of slavery. Abraham Lincoln, who had led the Union, had become President in 1861 but was assassinated in 1865.

Discovery and conquest

Exploration overseas

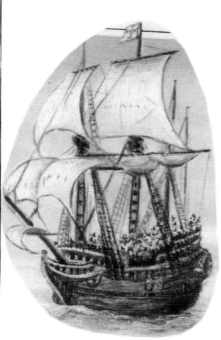

Henry the Navigator (1394-1460)

A Portuguese prince, born in Oporto, Henry the Navigator had a great interest in maritime exploration. He built an observatory and an academy of seamanship and navigation while, under his sponsorship, Portugal discovered the islands of Madeira and Porto Santo, established a monopoly of trade and conquest over the north-western coast of Africa, beyond Cape Bojador and eventually reached the Tropic of Cancer. His encouragement of voyages of discovery pioneered the 'Age of Exploration' and Lisbon became the meeting place for adventurous mariners.

Christopher Columbus (1451-1506)

Born in Genoa, Christopher Columbus sought a passage to India and Cathay by sailing west, a mission he set out to accomplish with religious zeal. Under the patronage of Ferdinand and Isabella of Spain, he embarked on his first voyage in the *Santa María* in August 1492. Despite many setbacks, storms, contrary winds, danger and near mutiny, on October 12, Columbus and his three ships landed in the West Indies. They had discovered the New World.

Columbus went on to discover Cuba, Guadeloupe and Puerto Rico, Trinidad and the mouth of the Orinoco in South America. In all, he made four voyages to the West but was unaware that what he had discovered was in fact a vast new continent.

Further exploration and conquest

In 1497 **John Cabot**, a Venetian navigator backed by Henry VII of England, reached Newfoundland, so discovering the mainland of North America, as opposed to the initial discovery of islands by Columbus

Vasco da Gama of Portugal reached India in 1498

Amerigo Vespucci, after whom America is named, explored the coast of Brazil from 1502 to 1503

In 1513 **Vasco Núñez de Balboa** discovered the Pacific

Hernando Cortès, the Spanish conquistador, conquered Mexico and the Aztecs from 1519, taking the

capital Tenochtitlán in 1521 with a small force of only 550 men

Ferdinand Magellan of Portugal discovered the route to the Pacific Ocean through the Magellan Strait in 1520. He was killed in the Philippines but the ship and crew went on to complete the first voyage right around the world

In 1531 **Francisco Pizarro** of Spain set out to undertake the conquest of Peru. With only 180 men, he crossed the Andes and — by a mixture of trickery, courage and brutality — he managed to capture Atahualpa, the

ruling Inca and to overwhelm his army of 30,000, thus establishing Spanish occupation

Sir Walter Raleigh (1552-1618) established the first colony in Virginia and explored the Guiana area of South America

In 1642 **Tasman** circumnavigated Australia and discovered New Zealand

James Cook (1728-1779) of Great Britain was the first navigator to sail south of the Antarctic Circle and to explore and chart much of the South Pacific, New Zealand and Australia

New concepts

Nicolas Copernicus (1473-1543)

A Polish astronomer, it was Copernicus who demonstrated and worked out in mathematical detail the concept of the solar system with the sun in the centre and planets revolving on their own axes, moving in orbit.

Galileo Galilei (1564-1642)

Galileo was the first modern scientist, that is, the first to combine experiment and theory in a truly structured way. He discovered the principles of falling bodies and pendulums and invented

the telescope — but it was his astronomical observations that had the greatest impact on our conception of the world, when, despite religious opposition, he finally established the Copernican theory of the universe.

Isaac Newton (1642-1727)

An English scientist and one of the greatest physicists in the history of science, Sir Isaac Newton, from his laws of motion went on to formulate the laws of gravity. He discovered many hitherto unknown facts about light and colour, in particular the composition of white light, and invented calculus, the most important mathematical innovation since those of Ancient Greece.

Charles Robert Darwin (1809-1882)

A great English naturalist, Charles Darwin's theory of Evolution by natural selection was published in *The Origin of Species* in 1859 after some twenty years of research and accummulation of evidence. There was an enormous outcry on its publication and, in fact, the controversy still continues, but his ideas opened up a completely new approach to the early history of the world.

New ideas invoke change

Knowledge spearheaded change. Often revolutionary ideas were initially ridiculed or opposed but eventually new truths were accepted and the way was clear for discovery and invention. A belief that the world was round provided the impetus for courageous exploration; understanding electricity created new platforms for invention; while awareness of bacteria and viruses revolutionized medicine.

History in action

Albert Einstein (1879-1955)

Born in Germany and later to become a Swiss and then an American citizen, Albert Einstein was a theoretical physicist whose ideas made the greatest changes to scientific thinking since Newton. He used the quantum theory to explain photo-electric effect and related mass to energy in an equation. His most famous *Theory of Special Relativity*, published in 1905, is one of the foundations of modern physics. This proposes that it is impossible to measure motion absolutely but only within a frame of reference involving time and space.

Splitting the atom

An atom is the smallest part of an element that can take part in a chemical reaction. Nuclear *fission* is the splitting of these atoms, as used in atomic bombs and nuclear reactors. Nuclear *fusion* occurs when nuclei of atoms join together, a process which occurs naturally in stars such as the sun and which is used in hydrogen bombs. Both fission and fusion release vast amounts of energy.

Shortly before the war German scientist Otto Hahn discovered that the atoms of uranium-235 would undergo fusion, creating a chain reaction and enormous release of energy. Dr Robert Oppenheimer at the University of California continued the basic research and went on to design and build the first atomic bomb.

By the 1950s US scientists were testing the hydrogen or thermonuclear bomb, as were scientists in the USSR, a situation which developed into an arms race. However, as the extremity of the long-term effects of such weapons on human life and the environment became more apparent, there was growing opposition to the lethal use of nuclear power. Its advantages as an energy source in peacetime also came under closer scrutiny following leaks from nuclear piles and power plants and the explosion at Chernobyl in Russia in 1986.

The Movies

Cinematic art is regarded by many as the most innovative art form of the twentieth century. From Thomas A Edison's Kinetoscope peep show in 1894 and the first motion-picture projection the following year, presented as part of a vaudeville show, creative film-making emerged as an exciting new medium, a popular source of entertainment and a powerful communication tool. The silent movie held sway for some twenty-five years or so and sound was not introduced until 1926. It was Al Jolson's appearance in *The Jazz Singer* that brought the Talkies into vogue. Technicolor was used first in 1922 and wide screens, with stereophonic sound appeared in 1952.

Early cinema highlights

Edison Kinetoscopic Record of a Sneeze was in 1884 the first motion picture copyrighted in the US.
The Great Train Robbery 1903 was one of the first US attempts to tell a story through film.
Quo Vadis 1912 was the first epic, lasting nearly two hours.
The Cabinet of Dr Caligari 1919 – the first horror film – was made in Germany and highly acclaimed.
The Four Horsemen of the Apocalypse and *The Sheikh* 1921 introduced Rudolph Valentino, the first screen lover to an ecstatic female audience.
The Kid 1921, *The Gold Rush* 1925 and *Modern Times* 1936 are just three of the many films created by Charlie Chaplin.
Mickey Mouse was launched by Walt Disney in 1927.

This is the great picture upon which the famous comedian has worked a whole year.
6 reels of Joy.
Charles Chaplin IN **"THE KID"**
Written and directed by Charles Chaplin
A First National ⊛ Attraction

Charlie Chaplin, actor, writer and director, is best known as the endearing tramp character

Little Caesar 1930 starred Edward G Robinson and was one of the first gangster films.
Blackmail 1931, directed by Alfred Hitchcock was the first British talking film.
The Gay Divorcee 1934 starred the new duo Fred Astaire and Ginger Rogers.
Snow White and the Seven Dwarfs 1938 was the first full-length animated cartoon.
Gone with the Wind 1939, starring Clark Gable and Vivien Leigh ran for 3 hours 45 minutes and broke all box-office records.
High Noon 1952, starring Gary Cooper was hailed as the definitive classic western.

Man on the Moon

On 21 July, 1969 American astronaut Neil Armstrong, commander of *Apollo II*, stepped off the ladder of the lunar module *Eagle* and became the first man on the moon. Marking this momentous event with the words, 'That's one small step for a man, one giant leap for mankind,' he was soon joined by Edwin 'Buzz' Aldrin to move slowly in the moon's low gravity. There they planted the American flag, took photographs and collected samples of dust and rock. A third astronaut, Michael Collins, remained in *Apollo II* in orbit around the moon until rejoined by Armstrong and Aldrin for their safe return home.

The infectious excitement of the astronauts was heightened by their sense of awe at being on the moon and their new view of the earth. This, together with the incredible technical expertise involved and the realisation of a 'science-fiction' dream, made the moon landing one of the most memorable moments in recent history.

The threads of discovery and struggle

Inventions

Early times (dates approximate)
4000 BC	Potters wheel	Mesopotamia
3500 BC	Bricks	Egypt & Assyria
3000 BC	Wheel	Asia
3000 BC	Plough	Egypt & Mesopotamia
1800 BC	Bathtub	Babylonia
1500 BC	Glass	Egypt
1500 BC	Glazed pottery	Mesopotamia
500 BC	Abacus	China
AD 105	Paper	China
AD 580	Suspension bridge	China
AD 780	Wood-block printing	China
AD 870	Windmills	Persia
AD 1000	Gunpowder	China
AD 1100	Magnetic compass	China

1300 to 1800
1440	Printing press	Gutenberg	Germany
1520	Rifle	Kotter	Germany
1590	Compound microscope	Janssen	Netherlands
1608	Telescope	Lippershey	Netherlands
1656	pendulum clock	Huygens	Netherlands
1698	Steam pump	Savery	England
1712	Steam engine	Newcomen	England
1714	Mercury thermometer	Fahrenheit*	Germany
1752	Lightning conductor	Franklin	USA
1764	Spinning Jenny	Hargreaves	England
1765	Condensing steam engine	Watt*	Scotland
1785	Power loom	Cartwright	England
1790	Sewing machine	Saint	England

1800 to 1900
1800	Electric battery	Volta*	Italy
1800	Lathe	Maudsley	England
1816	Bicycle	Sauerbronn	Germany
1823	Digital calculating machine	Babbage	England
1822	Camera	Niepce	France
1828	Blast furnace	Nielson	Scotland
1831	Dynamo	Faraday	England
1834	Reaping machine	McCormick	USA
1837	Telegraph	Morse*	USA
1846	Lock-stitch sewing machine	Howe	USA
1858	Refrigerator	Carré	France
1859	Internal combustion engine	Lenoir	France
1866	Dynamite	Nobel*	Sweden
1876	Telephone	Bell	Scotland
1879	Incandescent lamp	Edison	USA
1887	Gramophone	Berliner	Germany/USA
1887	Motor car engine	Daimler* & Benz	Germany
1892	Zip fastener	Judson	USA
1895	Wireless	Marconi	Italy
1897	Diesel engine	Diesel*	Germany
1898	Submarine	Holland	Ireland/USA
1888	Pneumatic tyre	Dunlop*	Scotland

The 20th century
1901	Vacuum cleaner	Booth	England
1903	Aeroplane	Wright brothers	USA
1913	Geiger counter	Geiger*	UK
1925	Television	Logie Baird	Scotland
	Frozen food process	Birdseye*	USA
1928	Penicillin	Sir Alexander Fleming	England
1930	Jet engine	Whittle	England
1935	Radar	Watson-Watt*	Scotland
	Nylon	Carothers	USA
1942	Nuclear chain reaction	Fermi	USA/Italy
1944	Ballpoint pen	Biro*	Argentina
	Automatic digital computer	Aiken	USA
1948	Transistor	Bardeen & others	USA
1955	Hovercraft	Cockerell	England
	Contraceptive pill	Pincus & others	USA
1960	Laser	Maiman	USA

* It is interesting to note how many proprietory names and commonplace words have been derived from inventors' names

Important wars and revolutions

Early times
431-404 BC	Peloponnesian War	Sparta, Corinth & Rome; Athens
264-146 BC	Punic Wars	Rome & Carthage

AD 1300 to 1800
1337-1453	Hundred Years War	France & England
1455-1485	Wars of the Roses	House of Lancaster & House of York
1562-1598	French Wars of Religion	France
1618-1648	Thirty Years War	France Sweden & Protestant German states; The Holy Roman Empire & Spain
1642-1649	The English Civil War	Parliamentarians & Royalists
1701-1713	Spanish Succession	England, Austria, Prussia, the Netherlands; France, Bavaria, Cologne, Mantua & Savoy
1740-1748	The Austrian Succession	Austria, Hungary, Britain & Holland; Bavaria, France, Poland, Prussia, Sardinia, Saxony & Spain
1756-1763	Seven Years War	Britain, Prussia & Hanover; Austria, France, Russia & Sweden
1775-1783	War of Independence	American colonies & Britain
1789-1795	French Revolution	factions within France
1792-1815	Napoleonic Wars	Austria, Britain, Prussia, Russia, Spain & Sweden; France

1800 to 1900
1846-1848	Mexican War	United States & Mexico
1853-1856	Crimean War	Britain, France, Sardinia & Turkey; Russia
1857	Indian Mutiny	India and Great Britain
1861-1865	American Civil War	The Union & the Confederacy
1870-1871	Franco-Prussian War	Prussia and German states: France
1898	Spanish-American War	USA & Spain
1899-1902	Boer War	Britain & Boer Republics
1894-1945	Chinese-Japanese Wars	China & Japan

The twentieth century
1900	Boxer Rebellion	China
1917	Russian Revolution	Russia
1904-1905	Russo-Japanese War	Japan & Russia
1912-1913	Balkan conflict	Turkey, Serbia, Bulgaria, Montenegro, Greece
1914-1918	World War I	Belgium, British Empire, France, Italy, Japan, Russia, Serbia & USA; Austria-Hungary, Bulgaria, Germany & Ottoman Empire
1935-1936	Abyssinian War	Italy & Abysinnia (Ethiopia)
1936-1939	Spanish Civil War	Fascists & Republicans
1939-1945	World War II	Australia, Belgium, Britain, Canada, China, Denmark, France, Greece, Netherlands, New Zealand, Norway, Poland, Russia, South Africa, USA & Yugoslavia; Bulgaria, Finland, Germany, Hungary, Italy, Japan & Romania
1950-1953	Korean War	South Korea & United Nations forces; North Korea & Chinese forces
1957-1975	Vietnam War	North & South Vietnam
1967	Six-Day War	Israel; Egypt, Syria, Jordan & Iraq
1967-1970	Nigerian Civil War	Federal government & Biafra
1971	Indo-Pakistan War	East Pakistan (Bangladesh) & India; West Pakistan
1973	October War	Israel & Jordan; Egypt, Syria, Iraq, Sudan, Saudi Arabia & Lebanon
1982	Falkland Islands	Britain & Argentina
1991	The Gulf War	America, Britain, Egypt France, Kuwait, Saudi Arabia, Syria; Iraq
1991-	Balkan Civil War	Serbians & Croatians

Exploration

Early times
c. 982	Eric the Red (Norse) visits Greenland	
c. 1000	Leif Ericson discovers North America	
c. 1272	Marco Polo visits China	

1300 to 1800
c. 1483	Diogo Cão discovers mouth of River Congo, Africa
1488	Bartolomew Diaz sails round Cape of Good Hope, Africa
1492	Christopher Columbus discovers West Indies
1497	John Cabot discovers Newfoundland
1498	Vasco da Gama reaches India via Cape Columbus visits South America
1499	Alonso de Ojeda explores Venezuela

1500 to 1800
1500	Pedro Alvares Cabral discovers Brazil
1502	Amerigo Vespucci explores Brazilian coast
1513	Vasco Núñez de Balboa finds Pacific Ocean
1519-21	Ferdinand Magellan circumnavigates world Hernando Cortés conquers Mexico
1520	Magellan discovers Tierra del Fuego, South America
1531	Francisco Pizarro conquers Peru
1534-6	Jacques Cartier explores St Lawrence River, North America
1541	Hernando de Soto discovers Mississippi River, North America Francisco de Orellana explores River Amazon, South America
1549	St Francis Xavier visits Japan
1596	Willem Barents discovers Spitsbergen
1603-9	Samuel de Champlain explores Canada
1610	Henry Hudson discovers Hudson Bay
1616	Willem Schouten discovers Cape Horn, South America
1642	Abel Tasman visits Australia & sights New Zealand
1728	Vitus Bering discovers Alaska
1769	James Cook visits New Zealand
1773	James Cook crosses Antarctic Circle
1789	Sir Alexander Mackenzie discovers Mackenzie River, North America
1795	Mungo Park explores River Niger, Africa

1800 to 1900
1818-21	Fabian von Bellinghausen circumnavigates Antarctica (sighted by Nathanial Palmer in 1820)
1828	Charles Sturt explores interior of Australia
1838-42	Charles Wilkes explores Antarctica
1851	David Livingstone discovers River Zambezi, Africa
1852-55	Heinrich Barth explores Sudan
1855	David Livingstone discovers Victoria Falls, Africa
1858	Richard Burton & John Speke discover Lake Tanganyika, Africa
1860-61	Robert Burke & William Wills cross from south to north of Australia
1868	Ferdinand Richtofen explores China
1877	Sir Henry Stanley traces River Congo
1888	Fridtjof Nansen explores Greenland

The twentieth century
1900	Duke of Abruzzi explores Arctic
1909	Robert E Peary reaches North Pole
1911	Roald Amundsen reaches South Pole 14 December
1912	Captain Robert Falcon Scott reaches South Pole 17 January but he and his party all perish on return journey
1953	Hilary and Tensing reach the summit of Mount Everest
1957-58	Sir Vivian Fuchs crosses Antarctica
1969	First men land on the Moon